PRAISE FOR *SACRED THIRST*

"Craig Barnes's compassionate spirit and pastor's heart shine through on page after page. In *Sacred Thirst*, Dr. Barnes helps the reader on a spiritual journey to understand the revelation of God."

—ELIZABETH H. DOLE
FORMER PRESIDENT OF THE AMERICAN RED CROSS

"Craig Barnes, one of our nation's leading pastors, not only addresses the doubts, fears, and questions that plague us all, but also points the way toward a more meaningful Christian life. With Craig's inspiring and guiding words, our hopes and expectations for the 'great hereafter' start with here and now."

—JOHN GLENN
FORMER U. S. SENATOR AND ASTRONAUT

"This is an important book for thirsty people. With wonderful stories and much practical wisdom, Craig Barnes teaches us new things about the only Water that can quench our deepest thirst."

—RICHARD J. MOUW
PRESIDENT AND PROFESSOR OF CHRISTIAN PHILOSOPHY,
FULLER THEOLOGICAL SEMINARY

"In *Sacred Thirst*, Craig Barnes connects the witness of Scripture to Jesus Christ with the realities of human life. As a pastor-theologian, he is well acquainted with both. I highly recommend this volume."

—THOMAS W. GILLESPIE
PRESIDENT AND PROFESSOR OF NEW TESTAMENT,
PRINCETON THEOLOGICAL SEMINARY

"Craig Barnes works on a quiet street, well away from the noisy, competitive religious marketplaces of our culture. Seek him out. He gives patient, sane, wise counsel for all of us who are thirsty for God. Men and women on their way to the well will welcome this book as a clean, cool drink of water."

—EUGENE H. PETERSON
PROFESSOR EMERITUS OF SPIRITUAL THEOLOGY,
REGENT COLLEGE, VANCOUVER, BC

"This is a wonderful book and deserves the widest audience possible. I have already read most of it through twice because I find it so spiritually perceptive and nourishing. Craig Barnes has a remarkable gift for not only describing the realities of hungers and needs in the human condition, but also for pointing to the ways and to the One who can truly satisfy. This remarkable book is not only challenging, but is also deeply encouraging."

—DR. ROBERTA HESTENES
MINISTER AT LARGE, WORLD VISION INTERNATIONAL

Also by M. Craig Barnes

Hustling God

SACRED THIRST

MEETING GOD
IN THE DESERT OF
OUR LONGINGS

M. Craig Barnes

ZondervanPublishingHouse
Grand Rapids, Michigan

A Division of HarperCollinsPublishers

We want to hear from you. Please send your comments about this book to us in care of the address below. Thank you.

ZondervanPublishingHouse
Grand Rapids, Michigan 49530
http://www.zondervan.com

Sacred Thirst
Copyright © 2001 by M. Craig Barnes
Requests for information should be addressed to:
ZondervanPublishingHouse
Grand Rapids, Michigan 49530

Library of Congress Cataloging-in-Publication Data
Barnes, M. Craig.
    Sacred thirst : meeting God in the desert of our longings / M. Craig Barnes.
      p.   cm.
    Includes bibliographical references.
    ISBN: 0-310-21955-8 (hardcover)
    1. Spiritual life—Christianity.   I. Title.
BV4501.2 B382857
248.4'851–dc21   00-046288

Published in association with the literary agency of Alive Communications, Inc., 7680 Goddard Street, Suite 200, Colorado Springs, CO 80920.

Interior design by Melissa Elenbaas
Printed in the United States of America

---

01 02 03 04 05 06 /❖ DC/ 10 9 8 7 6 5 4 3 2 1

For my daughter,
Lyndsey, the beloved,
with whom I am well pleased

CONTENTS

PART

1

THE THIRSTY CHRISTIAN

1

OUR PARCHED SOULS

The church was packed for Linda's funeral. On the front pew sat her parents, husband, and two children. I sat in the minister's bench directly in front of them and gazed into their faces as the Twenty-third Psalm was read.

This family was lost in heartbreaking grief. They were wondering the same thing everyone in grief wonders: How can the world go on so easily, as though nothing has happened? Linda was once a vibrant, loving, young mother, but now breast cancer had taken her away from us.

I tried to concentrate on the psalm, but a relentless sorrow kept piercing through. *The Lord is my shepherd, I shall not want. . . .* Except for Linda. I wanted Linda back.

When it came time for the eulogies, two of Linda's friends spoke first. They wept a bit as they described how much they loved Linda and how desperately they already missed her. The congregation and I expected these words and held up pretty well as we heard them. But the third eulogy was given by Linda's nine-year-old son. We weren't ready for what he had to say. It wouldn't have mattered if we had been. There was no defense against this moment.

I can still see him standing behind the podium, stretching up toward the microphone. Like a brave little soldier, he read dutifully from the paper in his hands: "Thank you for being here today to say good-bye to my mother, who has gone to heaven. I want you to know a couple of the things that my sister and I will miss about Mommy. We'll miss the way she always greeted us when we got home from school. She would be in the kitchen and we would run into her arms, and it felt good to be home. I'm going to miss that. At nighttime, when we had to go to bed, she would race us to our beds, then we'd jump in them and have tickling contests. And she would read us a story. I'm going to miss that too." Then he folded up his piece of paper, stuffed it into his pocket, and sat down.

As if that weren't enough to completely undo us, the tenor soloist began to sing softly, *Jesus, lover of my soul, let me to thy bosom fly.* The music gently found its way into the protected corners of every heart there. How could such tenderness wage war on all our defenses and illusions of immortality? By the time the song was done, we had surrendered to the sorrow.

Now it was my turn to speak.

But I couldn't. So I sat there in the silence, dabbing my eyes. Eventually, of course, I had to say something. I'm the pastor; it's my job to speak into the silence.

Sacred Silence

I've seen this silence before. It's created not only by little boys with broken hearts but also by lab reports announcing the presence of cancer, bosses trying to explain a downsizing, and notes on a dresser that say "I'm leaving." The silence is produced by gravestones, nursing homes late at night, children with dangerously high fevers, and coming across the Christmas stocking of a spouse who recently died. It can even be found on the heels of successes and achievements that are never quite what we thought they would be, leaving us empty and disappointed.

We hate this silence. It isn't the type that comes as a welcome relief from our chaotic lives. It's the silence that rips away the words we grope for in trying to explain life and to find hope.

Most of the time we're able to cover this silence with our cherished distractions. But occasionally something breaks through and hushes us with ultimate, difficult questions. These are the questions that push us to stare at the limits of our existence and ask, "Why are we here? What is really important? Is there anything to which we can cling in life?" In these quiet moments there's no escaping these questions. They stare us straight in the eye, daring us to say something—to say anything—that isn't foolish.

One day, a colleague at work tells you that his teenage son has just committed suicide. Stunned, you pause for a moment and finally stutter out, "I—I don't know what to say." Exactly. You've learned by now not to point out that he has two other wonderful children or that you're sure his son is in a much happier place or that your neighbor's kid committed suicide a while back. It would all sound completely asinine. Yet I am certain there are no human words that are any better.

Still, we cannot leave it at this, because our souls long to find some way of making sense of life. I sometimes think humanity's most heroic trait is that we refuse to let silence have the last word. We know that if *nothing* can be said, then our worst fears are true and there is no point or hope to life.

Even though we might not have intended to, we have now embarked on a great journey in search of a word that can fill the silence and make sense of life again. Some of us bring the search to church, wondering if maybe God has such a word.

Whenever I stand behind the pulpit to say, "Hear the word of the Lord," I can never say more than God says at this place on the journey. Many in the congregation hope that God's word will quickly get them out of this hard place where the silence is deafening. But when we are on a journey through a hard place with God, there are no shortcuts.

Silence is never more than an invitation to discover the limitation of all human words, even all religious words. It is not an answer or an explanation, it is not even a theology, but a person we are searching for. A sacred person. God himself, whom the Bible reveals as one God in three persons—Father, Son, and Holy Spirit.

All the words God spoke in the Old and New Testaments had as their purpose to draw us back to our true home in the midst of a triune fellowship into which we are adopted. This is the true "Holy Family" that comforts little boys who mourn their dead mothers and provides hope for cynical adults who long ago lost their way in the silence. Like a stream flowing through the desert, so does the Holy Spirit flow from the Father and the Son into our lives, carrying us, sometimes gently, sometimes in a torrent, but always home to God.

We can find this sacred river. But not unless we enter the silent desert.

THE INVITATION TO THE DESERT

The desert is one of the fundamental motifs used in both the Old and New Testaments to describe this difficult, speechless pilgrimage toward God. All of the patriarchs, Moses and the Hebrew people, Elijah, David, John the Baptist, Paul, and even Jesus had to go to the desert to find God.

No one in ancient society wanted to go to the desert. It was a parched, desolate place where people were convinced they would die. If they had to pass through a desert, they did it as quickly as possible, because it wouldn't be long before they would run out of resources. But the worst part of the desert was always the deafening silence. Human words don't last long out there, and divine words are as hard to find as a drop of water in the endless expanse of heat and sand.

When God finally did speak, his words appeared as a stream of water to a people whose souls had become as parched and silent as the dried-up desert in which they lived. When they attended to God's words and stayed by the stream in the desert, like deer who long for flowing streams, they found refreshment for their souls.[1] But if they allowed fear or grief to drown out God's words, they could turn back only to the silence of the parched desert.

Perhaps the most important thing to remember about the desert is that God never wants anyone to stay there. There is no easy way out, but one of the worst mistakes we can make is to get used to living in the dry places. The only point of going through the desert is to get to the Promised Land, where we are at home with God. And the only way to enter the land is to realize that the thirst we feel is actually a longing for the sacred.

Along the way in the desert, we may do a lot of things that lead us away from God and from the future he has prepared for us. Anything we do to turn away from God is what the Bible calls *sin*. Moreover, learning to turn in the right direction when we are tempted is one of our purposes for being in the desert in the first place. We sin by turning to other gods, by doubting the faithfulness of the true God, and by constantly complaining about how much we hate life in the desert. Still, our greatest sin is when we give up hope and stop looking for the stream along the way.

As the New Testament story goes, eventually we all became so lost in our desert of addictive despair that God had to do more than speak words to lead us through it. He had to *become* the Word. So on a silent, holy night the Word became flesh and lived among us, full of grace and truth. The Word's name was Jesus, the lover of our souls, the giver of living water. Nothing can separate us from his love—neither our grief nor our sin, not even our despair.

SAMARITAN SPIRITUALITY

Jesus gave his best explanation about living water to a Samaritan. The Samaritans were distant cousins of the Jews. The Samaritans believed in God, sort of, but they were not "orthodox." They had no interest in proper religion. When the king of Assyria defeated the ten northern tribes of Israel in the eighth century before Christ, he dispersed many of the Israelite residents to the far corners of his empire. They were never heard from again. Then the king shipped in citizens of other defeated nations to live where these "lost tribes" used to be.[2] But he left enough Israelites behind so that, in time, they intermarried with the new arrivals and blended their identities. The result was the Samaritans, a people with a bloodline that was anything but pure.

They were a spiritual people, but their religion was a mixture of Judaism and Hellenism. They were selective about what parts of the Hebrew Scriptures they followed, ignoring, for example, all of the writings of the prophets. But what offended the Jews most of all was that the Samaritans didn't worship at the temple in Jerusalem.[3]

In light of this deeply entrenched religious animosity, it is remarkable that Jesus announced his offer of life-giving water to a Samaritan woman.[4] We eventually learn that this woman had already had five husbands and that the man she was currently living with was not her husband. This was not the life she had planned. She knew all about the silence that resides on the other side of failed dreams. At noon, the hottest part of the day, she had quietly come to a well for water. But it wasn't just her throat that was parched.

This woman at the well certainly isn't the last "Samaritan" searching for something that will bring relief. Today there are countless spiritually thirsty people who will have nothing to do with our "orthodox" temples and churches.

Consider, for example, the man who wakes up Saturday morning delighted that he has the entire day free. Savoring a cup of Starbucks, he thinks about how to spend his day. Remembering that he has friends coming over for dinner and that there is nothing in the refrigerator, he plans a trip to the grocery store. Of course, the store is near the barber, so he might as well get his hair cut while he's out and about.

Thinking about how much he needs a haircut reminds him of his mother's nagging, which reminds him that her birthday is next week and that he still hasn't picked out a card. So he has to stop by the drugstore to get the card, which is near the shoe repair shop and the cleaners, and, come to think of it, he has to stop by both of those as well.

What he really wants is to get some exercise, which reminds him to check the play-off schedule for his favorite team, which reminds him how much his ex-wife despised sports. This reminds him that he still needs to call her lawyer, which makes him feel anxious about money, which reminds him that his credit cards are all maxed-out.

Suddenly his optimism about the day has evaporated—and he hasn't even left the kitchen! His free day has degenerated into a chaos of competing requirements for his life. He wonders how life ever became so complicated. He wonders, longingly, if there is something that will pull it all together for him. Maybe he should get married again. Maybe he should work harder or move to the coast. Or maybe, just maybe, he should check into this spirituality thing so many people are talking about these days.

Spirituality is about as hot as it gets today. All of the superchain bookstores have shelves upon shelves of books on spirituality. Amazon.com, the largest seller of books on the Internet, lists over nineteen hundred books just on angels alone. Spirituality is in the movies, seminars, magazines, and television. It's hard to keep track of how many "angel-to-the-rescue" TV shows are on the air. And spirituality is now acceptable conversation at any dinner party. William Buckley once commented, "It used to be that if you mentioned religion at a party you were never invited back. Now everyone stops their conversations to listen to you."

According to a recent Gallup poll, ninety-eight percent of all Americans pray, while ninety-six percent of all Americans believe in God. (I wonder who it is the other two percent are praying to.) Of those surveyed, ninety-three percent own Bibles, which is still the best-selling book in the country. But apparently we aren't reading these Bibles very carefully. Over half of us cannot recite the names of the four Gospels or name five of the Ten Commandments. Moreover, sixty percent of us do not attend worship, and sixty-one percent do not believe in the resurrection of the body. Sadly, ten percent think Joan of Arc was Noah's wife.[5]

In spite of society's current infatuation with spirituality, people are not becoming Bible scholars, embracing orthodox doctrine, or coming to worship in our "temples." In fact, hearing the word of God is not in style these days, merely yearning for it. Atheism is passé. No one really argues about whether or not God exists anymore. However, in its place is not biblical faith but a dream to find God, along with a hope that once we do, all the competing pieces will come back together. At least this seems to be what our "Saturday morning man" is thinking as he ponders his life over a cup of Starbucks coffee.

On a recent flight I sat next to someone who had been sent by his company, a major computer manufacturer, to a seminar on "spirituality in the family." He explained, "I don't think my manager really knows what this thing is all about. She just thinks I'll be more productive if things are happy at home. I don't know. Maybe it will help." This is precisely how so many of us think about spirituality: *Maybe it will help*. Having grown weary of constructing our lives with the things we find in this world, we think that perhaps pouring a little spirituality into the mix will help. Like the ancient Samaritans, many of us are making this mixture uncritically—a cup of New Age, a dash of ancient Gnosticism, a few tablespoons of self-help, even a bit of Bible for good measure.

Thus reporter Ruth Shalit observes, "Even as Americans absent themselves from the disciplines and encumbrances of traditional religion, angels have returned with a vengeance, but with less manifestation of faith than an objectification of a need; a spiritualization of psychology and sociology, a nostalgia for enchantment."[6] It is easy for those of us who have spent our lives in church to be cynical about this latest "Samaritan" interest in spiritual things, but it is more helpful to focus on the deeper issue. In the words of Shalit, the issue is the objectification of a need. In the words of a pastor, it is *a thirst for God.*

SOUL SADNESS

After worship one Sunday morning, a woman told me she appreciated a book I had written on finding God's love in the interruptions of life.[7] She said it was the best thing she had read since *The Bridges of Madison County.* Somewhat taken aback, I told her that hers was one of the more interesting reviews I had received, and then I pointed out that the two books really weren't saying the same thing. "Oh, I realize that," she responded, "but they both touched me so deeply." Well, there it is. Truth is now beside the point. The point is to be touched in that lonely, sad place of our souls. Perhaps a fantasy lover can reach us that deeply, we think. Maybe a loving God—just maybe.

One of the privileges a pastor enjoys is to be invited into some of the deepest chambers of people's lives. I am amazed at how often I find a lonely sadness hiding beneath layers and layers of success and respectability. The sadness I encounter is not depression, for these people really are functioning just fine. It's more of a quiet sorrow that has attached itself to the walls of the inner soul, a subdued sorrow that simply will not go away. Sometimes people attribute it to some specific grief or disappointment in their lives, but this sadness appears just as often in the lives of those who have experienced very little heartache in life.

We can relieve the pain it causes, at least for a time, but it isn't long before the sorrow returns. Some keep trying different cures to get rid of the sorrow, but many give up after a while and resign themselves to always being "a little sad at times." They give thanks that for the most part their lives are okay, and they regularly tell themselves they really can't complain. They go about their business like the Samaritan woman, who quietly made her solitary journey to the well. But late at night, when they can't sleep, they lie in bed staring at the ceiling, wondering why they really aren't all that happy.

One of the driving motivations behind the current fascination with spirituality is the felt need to find something, or someone, to do more than numb this sadness. We want it to go away. But nothing we have picked up in the desert so far can do this for us—not all of the materialism that abounds in our society, not all of our lofty achievements, not even our healthy marriages. One of the greatest stresses on marriage is that we ask it to do more than it's capable of doing. No human being can take away sadness. Not the spouse you have. Not the one you wish you had. A nagging sense of lonely sadness is a spiritual problem that requires a spiritual response.

Dick Peters recognizes this. Dick is a leader in our community who has, to use his words, "lived a charmed life." He has achieved more in his career than most people would ever dream of accomplishing. There are certainly more goals he could achieve in life, but none of them look all that interesting these days. Dick truly loves his wife and adores his two teenage sons. Yet after going on and on describing to me how wonderful his life is, Dick finally admitted, "I'm terrified that I might do something stupid real soon." He went on to explain that he wasn't interested in being just another pathetic victim of a midlife crisis, but he felt like he was being pulled toward something desperate that would certainly be self-destructive. "Sometimes at night," he told me, "my heart is beating so hard I can't sleep."

This is usually the point in the conversation when I start gently to make a referral to our church's counseling center. But Dick was already seeing an excellent therapist in our community. The counselor was beginning to think that his crisis was spiritual in origin. After Dick and I had talked for a while, I agreed with the therapist. Dick's issue was not clinical depression, but a despair that had left him distressingly sad. Now that he was at a place in his life where he could no longer outrun the sadness, he had no choice but to take on the despair that was causing it. Despair is invariably a spiritual issue. It is a hopelessness that emerges when we believe that there is no mystery left to our lives.

This sense of despair is one of the prevailing themes of contemporary society. Unlike previous generations that were preoccupied with survival, we have the luxury of staring into our morning coffee and asking ourselves why we are still so sad. Richard Ford, a rather typical postmodern novelist, observes, "It's exactly like when you were young and dreaming of your family's vacation; only when the trip was over, you were left with the empty husks of your dreams and the fear that that's mostly what life will be—the husks of your dreams lying around you. I suppose I will always fear that whatever *this* is, is *it*."[8]

When we arrive at the place in life where we discover that whatever this is, is it, we can either resign ourselves to the despair, which is exactly how we will end up dismantling our lives, or we can see this hopelessness as a yearning for the God who is not yet done creating our lives.[9]

THE DISTORTED IMAGE

When Albert Schweitzer went to Equatorial Africa and began speaking to people about the presence of God, one of the tribal chiefs said, "We knew someone passes on the edge of the forest, but we never knew his name." Everyone now seems to admit that someone passes on the edge of life, even if we don't know his name. Even though people have been trying to prove God's existence for thousands of years, I am still most convinced by the traces of God that have been left on the human soul.

John Calvin, the sixteenth-century Protestant Reformer, claimed that the image of God remains on our souls; yet because we have so corrupted the image by sin, it is hard to recognize it in us. In the silent moments, though, there is still enough of the image left for us to realize that we thirst for something. But Calvin is right. The image is just too distorted to recognize who it is we are thirsting for. So we keep searching and searching until, like the Samaritan woman, we may find ourselves just quietly going through the motions of life, doubting we will ever find what our souls crave.

When today's "Samaritans" come to me to talk about their struggles to believe in God, I no longer find that the significant block to faith is intellectual doubt. These days it seems that people are prevented from believing more by their despair than by their doubt—and the younger they are, the more true this seems to be. Young people today hope for little—and expect less. In large measure, this is also true about their perspectives on the rest of life. They expect little from politics, about which it has now become stylish to be cynical. They expect little from an economy that hasn't resulted in making their parents happy, in spite of all the money they earned in the stock market. And they expect very, very little from organized religion, which is by and large as preoccupied with self-maintenance today as were the keepers of the temple in Jerusalem a couple of thousand years ago.

It doesn't matter whether it's a young person who is having a hard time getting excited about all that contemporary society promises them, a middle-aged woman who has gone through five husbands, or an old man disillusioned about the choices he's made throughout his life—the mark of all "Samaritans" is their refusal to come to the temple to find hope. Stubbornly they search for God in other places. And the last thing any self-respecting Samaritan is ever going to claim today is that he or she has found God. What *is* in fashion is merely yearning for him.

Thirsty in the Temple

The Samaritan woman is the embodiment of this yearning. To her great surprise, Jesus, a Jewish man, was sitting at the well when she arrived. Even more amazingly, he began to speak to her about being thirsty. She must have wondered, *What is he doing here? Has he lost his way? Has he lost his faith that he would dare talk to me?* At this time Jewish men would not even talk with Jewish women in public, let alone their Samaritan counterparts. In fact, there was a group of Pharisees known as "the bruised and the bleeding," so named because they would close their eyes whenever they saw a woman in public, even if it meant walking into a building and breaking their noses. In contrast to those who used religion to insulate themselves from the world, Jesus was determined to engage this woman in a conversation about her great thirst.

At first their discussion didn't go very well. Not only did the woman fail to recognize who it was she was talking to, she didn't understand what Jesus was talking about. She was missing all the metaphors. Jesus spelled it out as clearly as he could: "Everyone who drinks of this water will be thirsty again, but those who drink of the water that I will give them will never be thirsty. The water that I will give will become in them a spring of water gushing up to eternal life."[10] "Great!" the woman responded, "Give me this water so I don't have to keep coming to this well."

We who are familiar with this story want to jump in and interject, "You just don't get it, woman. Jesus isn't talking about your physical thirst, but your spiritual thirst." Exactly. We know that. So why do we still experience so much spiritual thirst?

Unlike the Samaritan woman, most of us do know who Jesus is. We know all about the cross and the resurrection. We have accepted his gift of forgiveness for our sins, been baptized, and joined the church. We may even serve on a committee or volunteer in church missions. We, at least, are not Samaritans. We even love the temple. But we still yearn for something more. We yearn for something more in our relationships and families. We yearn for something more in our jobs and sense of purpose. We yearn, most of all, for something more in our experience of God.

George Barna, one of the leading researchers on church and religious issues, recently published statistics showing that seventy-five million people attend church every Sunday. But less than one-third of these people believe they interacted with God during the worship service, and over one-third say they have never experienced God's presence.[11] That is amazing. But one statistic Barna didn't cite is even more striking: One hundred percent of us thirst for more of God than what we now have.

Like the woman at the well, sooner or later, perhaps in a quiet, reflective moment, we must all come to terms with the honest truth that we are looking for more than we've found thus far. We certainly don't resemble the Samaritan woman. We keep our marriages to a minimum, and we hold down respectable jobs and pay our bills on time. We may look pretty respectable and orthodox. But still our souls are so very thirsty.

Perhaps your prayer life has dried up, or in spite of your best efforts you still are not making much of a difference in anyone's life, or maybe you've lost all the joy, all the passion, in your life. You have the same sadness buried in your soul as all those Samaritans had. You may have a head full of knowledge about God, but you still yearn to experience something sacred, something that will at long last calm the ache from deep within. As this story unfolds, take your place next to this Samaritan woman.

It's part of my pastoral calling to look closely at the lives of those who go to church. They all clean up pretty nicely on Sunday morning. But just below the surface of their navy-blue suits and colorful dresses lie souls that are not nearly so tidy. On a typical Sunday in our church, I sit facing the congregation while the choir sings the anthem before the sermon. I gaze into the faces of people I know and love. I see the elder whose marriage is hanging on by a thread. Next to him is the Sunday school teacher whose daughter was arrested last week for driving under the influence of alcohol. Two pews behind them is the church's newest widow, who is wondering how she will survive sitting in church alone for the first time in forty years. She happens to be sitting next to a young couple who desperately want to be parents, but not a single one of the fertility treatments seems to be helping. The details may change as I look from face to face, but the essential story remains the same. They are all thirsty.

My job is to remember that what we are struggling with is not just our families and jobs. No, the stakes are much higher than that. The real struggle is with our parched souls. We were created with a need to satisfy our physical thirst, and every morning of our lives we are reminded of this thirst. But this physical thirst is a symbol, maybe even a sacrament, that points to the deeper spiritual thirst of the soul. So also is our longing for better families and more satisfying jobs a symbol of our deeper yearning to be a part of the family and the mission of God. We simply cannot satisfy the thirst of our souls by pouring on new relationships, experiences, achievements, or careers.

As the Samaritan woman discovered, it doesn't matter how many times we may try to rearrange our relationships and reorder our lives. Until we find relief for the soul, everything else will be nothing more than a distraction—a very temporary one at that—from our fundamental craving for living water.

Most of us haven't gone through five spouses, but we have gone through five jobs, five moves, five weight-loss programs, or five churches—and still the insatiable thirst continues. We will never find what we are looking for in the things we pick up along the way. Not even the religious things. Not even important things like relationships. All of these things will leave our souls empty if we try to force them to satisfy our thirst. The true object of our search is nothing less than an encounter with the Holy One.

CHAPTER 2

RIGHT ANSWERS AREN'T ENOUGH

My father pastored a church on Long Island that he and my mother had started pretty much from scratch. We met in the basement of a home for quite a while, but after years of hard work the growing congregation was finally able to buy a small, old church building. Eventually we built and moved into a big brick church.

This was years before anyone had heard of a "seeker church," but most of the people who came to our church were definitely of the seeking variety. They had little church background and knew next to nothing about the Bible, worship, or the fundamentalism my father was eager to serve them.

The music of this church was far from contemporary or even seeker-friendly. We sang mostly "blood-and-guts" hymns, as my friends called them. I can still hear Mother (I always sat next to her) singing the alto part as I chirped along, *There is a fountain filled with blood drawn from Immanuel's veins; and sinners plunged beneath that flood lose all their guilty stains.* So it wasn't the music that brought people in.

Nor do I think anyone came to our church because of my father's seeker-sensitive sermons, which really weren't very sensitive to

anyone, least of all seekers. Dad wasn't really a fire-and-brimstone
kind of person, but he did like talking about the devil quite a bit. Once
a year, for Youth Sunday, he would pull out his favorite sermon, "The
Devil's Toolbox." He used a Craftsman toolbox which he had painted
red. Inside he had all the tools the devil might use to tear apart someone's life: an empty bottle of booze, a deck of cards, a pack of ciga-
rettes, an astrology book, a hypodermic needle, a set of brass
knuckles, and a pornographic magazine with certain parts of the
cover blacked out. Clearly, it was an effective sermon, because I
remember it better than most of the sermons *I've* given.

He also loved to tell the Old Testament stories of people like
Joshua, David, Gideon, and Naaman the Syrian captain. My dad's
faith was of the muscular variety that stressed trying hard—really
hard—"to come out from among them and be different." Kids
were told to avoid movies and school dances, while adults were
warned to avoid just about everything but worship, Bible study,
and Wednesday evening prayer meeting. I guess you might say
Dad wasn't about to make the Christian life easy.

Why, then, did so many people flock to this church, meet Jesus
as their Savior there, and begin to live a different life? I think it was
mostly because there was something about my parents that was
attractive to the worn-out souls in our community. It wasn't Mom
and Dad's personalities, which were as flawed as the sinners who
came to them. But my parents knew how to find Jesus and his living water. They talked about him, pointed to him, and led others to
the well every day of their ministry. Along the way, thirsty alcoholics
and drug addicts turned into choir members. Welfare recipients found
a reason to stand on their own feet again. People with money became
good stewards. And my brother and I discovered a vision that led us
to dedicate our own lives to the family business of serving the church.

I now disagree with many of my father's ideas about the faith. I
think my answers to the questions people ask are better than the
ones I heard from his pulpit. Still, he and Mom taught me from an
early age that much of this really misses the mark. When it comes
to caring for parched souls, having the right answers is never enough.

One particularly memorable lesson took root when I was about
twelve, suffering through Mrs. Shirmer's Sunday school class. Mrs.
Shirmer was pretty typical of the people attracted to our church.

She had no idea what the Bible said, but, since very few in the church did, Dad went ahead and asked her to teach. One morning she enthusiastically proclaimed to our class that Noah and his family had stayed in the ark during a terrible storm that lasted four whole days and nights. I rudely interrupted, "It was *forty* days and nights, which, as anybody knows, is what it takes to wipe out the world." Mrs. Shirmer ran out of the class crying. Later, when my mother was scolding me for my behavior, I protested that I was right. "No you weren't, Craig," Mom replied, "and I hope someday you'll understand that."

Not too many months later my father taught me another lesson in this difficult concept. After Communion worship services, Johnny Burke and I loved to run to the back room, where we would wolf down the leftover juice and broken crackers. One night after Communion, Johnny got there before I did and consumed all of the "spoils" without me. Without thinking (obviously), I began to recite some of the verses my dad made me memorize: "For he that eateth and drinketh unworthily, eateth and drinketh damnation to himself, not discerning the Lord's body. For this cause many are weak and sickly among you, and many sleep."[1] (This is the danger of having children memorize too much Scripture.) Johnny asked me what these verses meant, so I explained that he would come down with polio by midnight. It was the worst thing I could think of. Later that night Mrs. Burke called our home to say that her son was crying uncontrollably, and she asked my father to come right over. He did, and when Dad got home we had another "talk" about rightly handling the word of truth.

What my parents were trying to get into my pharisaical little mind was that the point of the church's ministry isn't to dole out a lot of verses and proclaim a lot of answers, but to draw people to the love of Jesus Christ. My parents knew tons of answers. But they had seen a lot of Samaritans in various stages of crisis, and they understood that people are saved not by *what* they know but by *who* they know.

JESUS IS A WHO, NOT A WHAT

It is significant that during Jesus' conversation with the Samaritan woman at the well he didn't try to convert her to Judaism, or even to Christianity. He just wanted to give her the only thing that would satisfy her thirst.

It is the nature of religions to systematize their beliefs into theological affirmations that make sense of their faith. For the church, this means obeying the second part of the Great Commission: to teach people to obey everything that Jesus commanded us.[2] Since, however, we often disagree in our interpretations of what Jesus and the Bible teach us, we also disagree concerning what we should teach others. This accounts for the great variety of denominations, theological traditions, and churches today. These disagreements are important and worthy of debate, but in the end they are all second-order issues. The first order of the church, found in the first part of the Great Commission, is to go and make disciples of all nations.

We are all too often more comfortable with the second order (that is, to teach), so we frequently try to make it our first order of priority. In short, we keep presenting Jesus as a *what* before we introduce him as a *who*. We tell people that Jesus, as the sinless Lamb of God, is the necessary sacrifice for our sins and that we will never make it to heaven unless we accept his offer of complete forgiveness. This is, to be sure, a critically important affirmation about Jesus' function in our salvation, but it is still second-order talk. No one can understand the power of any of this until he or she first meets Jesus and obeys his primary order to follow him as a disciple.

Granted, the typical approach to "disciple making" today encourages people to have a personal relationship with Jesus Christ (the first order), but we then devote enormous amounts of time and energy to teaching them things about Jesus. We seem to be not as careful to show them ways of continuing to know Jesus ever more deeply. Knowing about Jesus is not the same as knowing him.

This form of disciple making is something like falling in love with someone, then spending the rest of one's life reading his or her résumé. This approach will never ultimately satisfy the thirsty people in our churches who know a great deal of theology but who yearn to fall in love with Jesus once again.

When the first disciples encountered Jesus they didn't understand much about his role in their salvation. Yet there was something so compelling about this man that they were willing to drop everything in order to follow him. For the next three years they caught glimpses, albeit confusing glimpses, of his mighty work in bringing heaven and earth back together, but it is clear they were never following a theological concept. Every time they thought they had Jesus figured out, he disappointed, and further confused, them. One gains the distinct impression that whenever Jesus would offer them another insight into his function, afterwards they would look at one another and say, "Did you understand that? I didn't get it. I never know what he's talking about." But through it all they continued to follow this person they could not understand. Why? Because the most important thing was not what they understood, but who they were following.

When we love someone, as the disciples loved Jesus, we are frequently surprised and even confused. Thus we are told that when the disciples found Jesus talking with this Samaritan woman, they "were astonished."[3] They and many others were also astonished at Jesus' teaching and at his power to heal, as well as confounded beyond words by his resurrection from the dead.

This element of astonishment is precisely what is missing in so many of us in the church today. We have completed all of the fill-in-the-blank Bible study workbooks and learned all the Christian answers to questions about every conceivable topic. We subscribe to Christian magazines, listen to Christian radio stations, date Christian people, and advocate for the Christian worldview in culture and politics. All of this has the effect of turning the word *Christian* into an adjective—which is something the Bible never does. What is even more dangerous, our preoccupation with "Christianizing" Jesus codifies and packages a person, who can never be easily contained. The bottom line is this: If we are not astonished by Jesus, we are following something other than the person described in the Bible.

When we agree to follow Jesus, we find that he always leads us outside the confines of our religious boxes. He was killed precisely because he defied the right answers and the expectations of the religious leaders in Jerusalem. Jesus referred to God as his Father, which none of the other messiah-types had dared to do. He called people to righteousness, then unmasked the hypocrisy of those who made a profession out of acting righteous. He hung around with sinners who wouldn't be caught dead in a synagogue, then told them to go and sin no more. And because Jesus never gave the religious leaders the expected answers to worn-out questions, they had to get rid of him. If the New Testament Gospels make anything clear, it is this: Jesus Christ is exactly who we need in our lives, and he is never the person we expect.

However, as my fundamentalist father would have reminded me, the New Testament also declares that there are clear and definite implications to knowing Jesus Christ. Of course there are. According to the writers of Scripture, knowing Jesus carries implications for how we live, what we do with our money, who we sleep with, and how we spend our fleeting days. But the biblical writers' authority to make these claims was rooted in their personal encounter with Jesus Christ. The apostles' teaching will never become a source of spirituality for us apart from our own daily surprising encounter with Jesus as well.

FINDING GOD IN THE WRONG ANSWERS

At the end of the Great Commission Jesus promised to be with us always, even to the very end. But the Son of God is not simply riding around in our backpacks, waiting for us to take him into the world. Through his Spirit Jesus is at work, even in parts of the world where people are doing and believing things that are, "theologically" speaking, flat-out wrong. When we follow Jesus to these places, armed with our "better" answers, we face a theological crisis. What is Jesus doing over there, on the wrong side, when we're knocking ourselves out to defend the "right" position?

For example, in the West Bank (the territory between Israel and Jordan) an evangelical priest named Father Emil Salyata is in charge of all the Catholic schools for Palestinian children. When I visited him recently, he told me that most of the children who come to his schools are Muslim. Still, they sit through all of the religious classes and chapels, participate in the Mass, memorize Scripture verses, sing the songs, and learn to love Jesus Christ. Some can explain Jesus' suffering on the cross just as well as children in my own church. Amazed, I exclaimed, "But I thought Muslims couldn't become Christians." Father Salyata's eyes grew

big as he said, "Oh, I would never make them Christians. I just
want them to follow Jesus Christ as their Lord and Savior."

This is more than a simple semantic distinction. In his country,
as in many others, *Muslim* and *Christian* are political identities.
Rather than institutionalizing Jesus into one of the competing fac-
tions, Father Emil witnesses to Jesus' presence among people who
are formally not only not Catholics but aren't even Christians.
Okay, but now I have a theological problem: Can Jesus be in the
heart of Muslims?

Like the disciples before me, I am discovering that the further
I travel out into the world the more astonished I become about
what Jesus is doing. After Jesus gave his commission and ascended
into heaven, his disciples became his apostles (his sent-out ones),
who were pushed further and further into the world. Along the
way the church grew, and the gospel became more bewildering.

The apostle Peter, for example, had to give up cherished beliefs
about who can receive the gospel of Jesus Christ. Once Peter was
at a friend's house by the Mediterranean Sea, and he went up on
the flat roof to pray and to be alone with God.[4] Peter was hungry,
but the noon meal was not yet ready. Suddenly Peter saw a vision:
a large sheet descending from heaven, containing all kinds of animals, reptiles, and birds. Then a voice from heaven commanded,
"Get up, Peter. Kill and eat." Peter responded, "I can't do that! I'm
a kosher Jew. We don't eat things that are unclean." The Lord
interrupted, asking, "Who do you think made these animals you're
calling unclean?"[5]

We are told that while Peter was wondering just what this
vision meant, he was prompted to go to the entrance of the house.
At the door were the servants of a Roman centurion named
Cornelius, who was not only a Gentile but an officer of the
Romans—the oppressors of the Jews. The Holy Spirit told Peter to
go with these men to Cornelius's home in Caesarea.

Now, if I had been Peter on my way to Caesarea, I would have
been wondering, *Why am I taking God to my enemy?* But when we are
introduced to Cornelius, we learn that he was "a devout man who
feared God with all his household; he gave alms generously to the
people and prayed constantly to God."[6] Peter didn't take God to
Cornelius. God could get to Cornelius on his own. So the question

is not, Can Cornelius find God? The question is this: Can those of us who hang out in the church find God as he continues to work beyond our doors? In fact, this is not the story of Cornelius's conversion to God; it is the story of Peter's conversion back to the world God still loves.

What we believe the right positions to be on any of the pressing debates of our society really does not matter in the end; the church must always be careful to avoid assuming that God can be contained within the rightness of these positions. Was it right for the Roman soldiers to occupy Israel? Certainly not, according to good Jews like Peter. But this did not prevent God from caring enough about Cornelius to send Peter to him. Presumably the very idea of entering this Gentile's house revolted Peter as much as the thought of eating those unclean animals had. He had worked so hard to avoid being defiled so that he could please the God who was now "defiling" himself by communing with Cornelius. What in the world was God doing with Cornelius?

The question bears asking: What is God doing with the people who are working against us on all of the important moral issues that divide our country? God is not there to be in solidarity with them or to condone their positions. No, he's there for the same reason he is with us—to offer the living water that our dried-out souls desperately crave. Does this mean that their positions aren't morally wrong? Not at all. But it does mean that it is never enough for us simply to be right if we want to know the God who has a passion for finding all of his lost creatures. Until we see God from the perspective of our enemies, we will never have seen enough of him.

Getting this other glimpse of God changes everything about us. We cannot see God differently and fail to be transformed by the process. Peter could never be the same after this experience with Cornelius. Later, when Paul was challenged by some in Jerusalem for his ministry with the Gentiles, it was Peter who came to his defense.[7] Why? Because his vision of the church, and even the size of his heart, simply had to grow once he had seen more of God.

Peter had come to realize that he could not simply assume that his position accurately or even adequately represented God's position. Likewise, when someone told Abraham Lincoln that God was on the side of the North in the Civil War, he responded, "Let us simply pray that *we* are on the side of God." Lincoln had a vision of God that transcended the "rightness" of his own position on the war—a vision he discovered by understanding that the churches of both the North and the South "read the same Bible, and pray to the same God, and each invokes his aid against the other.... The prayers of both could not be answered; and that of neither has been answered fully. The Almighty has his own purposes."[8]

I often think of these words when I speak to couples who have come to see me because their marriage is in serious trouble. Too many of us spend a lot of time arguing about who is right and who is wrong, and it never gets us anywhere in the end. Frankly, most of the time one person is more right than the other, but recognizing and admitting this still doesn't help. The breakthrough in the stalemate will not come until they both realize that there is a sacred mystery at work in the other person's life. When they make this discovery, they become thirsty to discover more of the God they see at work in the other person; it is then that they are able to fall in love again.

In essence it's just the same lesson my parents taught me a long time ago: When you are in a theological, political, or even marital crisis, it's not *what* you know that will save you, but *who* you know. The Almighty does have his own purpose: to bring relief to our parched souls. Often he achieves this purpose by demonstrating just how unsatisfying it is to be dead-right.

Spiritual Hitchhiking

These days many thirsty Protestants, disenchanted with the stale orthodoxy in which they were raised, have begun to glean insights for their faith from Roman Catholicism. Most do not convert to this tradition but rather borrow freely from it as a way of finding what has been missing as a result of all their emphasis on right answers. They are tired of learning about God, and they're ready for a less dogmatic, more soulful experience of him.

Books by Henri Nouwen, Thomas Merton, Brother Lawrence, Saint John of the Cross, and his teacher Teresa of Avila now line the shelves of most Christian bookstores. (There's the adjective again. Really now, how can a bookstore be Christian?) Twenty years ago one would have had to go to the library or the cramped book room of a Catholic church to find these titles.

Most Protestant seminaries now offer classes and degree programs in "Spiritual Direction" and "Mentoring" because the market demands them. Their Catholic counterparts and monasteries organize spiritual retreats where one can check in and be a monk for a day.

New forms of worship have also proliferated. Leading the way is music that provides the heart immediate access to God without spending much time in the mind. The mind we have tried, yet we are still restless to encounter sacredness. Furthermore, having spent most of their lives learning the right words to use in prayer, Protestants who are on the cutting edge today are learning to pray without words, to find our way to the center where we listen to the Spirit who prays on our behalf with utterances too deep for human words.

Some have said that all of this is just the latest fad in the perpetual renewal movements that come and go within the church. We've tried revivalism, charismatic movements, faith-at-work activities, small groups, community building, and social concern programs, so why not try Catholic spirituality? These critics will also point out that Protestants are adopting aspects of the Catholic tradition they like while ignoring the theological assumptions that lie behind this spirituality, as well as spurning the power of their own tradition. (For example, the Protestant Reformation was built around such axioms as the power of God's Word, the Bible, to transform our lives.)

I think the critics are right about people tending to ignore the contradictions between Catholicism and Protestantism. Still, because their passion, their vigorous yearning, is to find something richer than orthodoxy, it should not surprise us that few are concerned about this inconsistency.

The critics are not right, however, to write all this off as a mere fad. None of the renewal movements we have seen in recent church history are fads in the sense of a fashion that comes and goes. All of them are actually alive and well in the church today, and it certainly appears that the Catholic and mystical contributions to our search for living water will be around for a long time to come. Still, the cynics who say this is not the last renewal movement we will see are clearly right. There will be others. There have always been and always will be movements to renew the church—movements that seem to emerge whenever the church has too many words and not enough vision.

I realize that by the time people walk into church on Sunday morning, they have been bombarded with words all week long. Words were used to sell them things they don't really need, to motivate them to do more, to manipulate, evaluate, and hurt them. Then, when I climb into the pulpit, what do I say? "Hear the word of the Lord." Many in the pews must be thinking, "Oh, no. Now what does God want from me?" Knowing this, I must be sure not to unload a barrage of words about God or about our responsibilities. I have to remember that the first order of business is to present the Word made flesh in Jesus. Whenever the church forgets to do that, these helpful renewal movements begin to break out. They are God's great gifts to help us recover our balance in the faith.

King David, who was described as a man after God's own heart, claimed that there was one thing he sought from the Lord: to "live in the house of the LORD all the days of my life, to behold the beauty of the LORD, and to inquire in his temple."[9] David has more than corporate worship in mind, for he wants to live every day in the presence of a God he can both behold and explore. Traditionally, the Catholic church has done a better job teaching its laypeople to behold God's beauty, while Protestants have tended to emphasize the inquiring part. But according to David, both are necessary. If we spend too much time inquiring about God, it is only a matter of time before the soul longs for a more aesthetic experience of beholding God's beauty.

Our faith has a wonderful self-correcting device built into it. As Jesus taught the woman at the well, this correction is our need to worship God in both spirit and in truth. If we are too preoccupied with defining the truth as "right answers," our parched souls will yearn for an encounter with God that can be experienced only through the spirit. If we become too enchanted with the spiritual journey for its own sake, then our souls will feel untethered until they return to the often hard truth of Jesus Christ.

Balance spirit & truth

We have labels for both of these extremes. Being consumed with the spiritual to the point of ignoring the biblical truths by which we must live creates *Gnosticism*, while ignoring the spiritual produces *thirstiness*. These days most of us in the Protestant church are closer to thirstiness than to Gnosticism. To be sure, we may be in danger of becoming Gnostics, like the many people who search for spirituality outside of biblical faith today; should that happen, however, I suspect we will see a revival in biblical teaching—not so much because I trust the church to correct its excesses, but because I trust God to do so. In the meantime, let us honor this latest interest in mystical spirituality, if for no other reason than because it reflects the need of the soul to possess something more than right answers.

MY FALLING STAR

When I was a little boy, I loved to visit my grandparents, who lived out in the country. I was there one night, when I glimpsed a shooting star. I ran into the house to tell my grandmother, who said it meant that if I made a wish it would come true. My eyes grew wide as I asked, "Really?" Then I told my grandfather about the shooting star. He explained it meant someone had just died and gone to heaven. My eyes grew even wider, and I exclaimed, "REALLY?" Finally, I told my older brother. He said he had just studied all that stuff in school, and so he began to explain about supernovas, trajectories of light, and light-years. "Oh," I replied. The wonder and the mystery had disappeared; I was now the disillusioned recipient of the right answer.

As a pastor, I've discovered that when people occupy the pews on Sunday morning, they are praying to discover something that will allow them to recover their childlike ability to ask, "REALLY?" The last thing people need from the church is more information that causes them to say, "Oh."

CHAPTER 3

A STRANGER IN COMMUNITY

Sooner or later you will feel like a stranger in church. It's only a matter of time. It will happen not just because someone there will do something to hurt and alienate you. More important, it will happen because the day will come when you realize that not even the church can satisfy your thirsty soul. That's the day you'll begin to wander off spiritually.

Because the parched soul is such an intense place, it is difficult, and relatively rare, to spend enough time in it to recognize its yearnings. So we are confused about why we feel agitated at church. Needing to find some rationale for our unhappiness and our feelings of estrangement, we look for flaws in the church. Finding them isn't hard.

HOW YOU LOSE COMMUNITY

The church is supposed to be a place where we can find God's grace in life. But like every other institution, it is often more worried about itself than concerned about the individuals within it. It will not always be gracious. When your church hurts you, at that moment you are as dis-graced as the Samaritan woman who was left alone to undertake a lonely search for living water in the desert of her own soul.

This loneliness can be unbearable when it occurs in a church where you once felt very much at home. You gave your heart to this congregation. You raised your kids in its Sunday school; you may have had a loved one's funeral in its sanctuary. So many identity-shaping memories were created there—which is precisely why it hurts so much to sit in church feeling like a familiar stranger.

Usually it takes more than one bad experience to leave you alienated from the church, but when the last one occurs, it is easiest to blame it for all your frustration. If people are dismayed at the intensity of your reaction, it's because they don't know about your other unresolved hurts inflicted by the church. Perhaps you don't even remember them all, but hurt is one of those things that doesn't improve with time. It just waits, not far below the surface, for a chance to escape. And escape it does—when one or more of the following triggers occur:

Conflict

Changes you just knew were all wrong were introduced into the church. You tried to resist them, and you pleaded your case, but when it came time for voting, you lost. You interpreted it as a vote of confidence for the leadership and a lack of confidence in you. Because of your many years of dedicated service, you were sure people would give you more respect. Even if later it were to become apparent to everyone that you were right, you don't think you'd be able to get over the realization that people did not trust your wisdom. *So,* you began thinking, *maybe it's time to step aside and let the newcomers lead the church in the wrong direction.*

To make matters worse, on the pathway that led to the vote some terrible things were said that you just can't forget. Lord knows, you've tried to forgive and enter again into the life of the community, but every time you see someone leading in worship or chitchatting informally in the church halls, all you can think about are the horrid rumors this person spread about you.

When I visit a few of our older members in their homes, it generally isn't long before they start talking about an old conflict in the church. It may have taken place twenty years ago, but they speak about it as though it had happened yesterday. Why? Because it was the moment when they no longer felt that the church was a ministry of grace to them. Since then, these folks have continued to worship, off and on, but they have never really felt at home in the church again.

The New Pastor

You loved your old pastor, who retired several months ago, but when the new pastor came on board, you resolved to give him a fair try. However, his sermons just don't connect with you. Most of the time you can't figure out the point, and when you do get it, you can't believe how irrelevant it is.

Reminding yourself that the church is more than its preaching, you try to hang in there a while longer. But before long the pastor not only preaches bad sermons but starts to make bad decisions about the church's ministry. Or maybe you were hoping for different decisions. Worst of all, perhaps there are *no* decisions—just a lot of elder retreats and nebulous vision statements. You ask yourself, "When are we going to get a real leader in this church again?"

Compassion Failure

When you were suffering through a painful crisis, no one from the church came to help. Yet you can hardly count the times you took a meal to the home of a new widow in the church, or the times you stayed late into the night at a church committee meeting! But when you were in the hospital, no one from the church came to see you. Or when your father died, no one bothered to call to express their compassion. Or perhaps you hadn't attended worship services for two months, and no one even noticed that you weren't there.

You wonder if anyone in this church ever cared about you; maybe you feel like they've just been using you for cheap volunteer labor. Then, a few months later, when you hear someone at church talk about its outstanding caring ministry, you want to throw up.

Inaccessible Music

The worship music at your church is too thin, or perhaps it's too dull. You hate it, and you find that the worship services never really usher you into God's presence. The whole service is like an airplane that makes a lot of noise as it chugs down the runway but never takes off.

Dissatisfaction with worship music is one of the most common reasons people give for feeling estranged from their spiritual communities. Because music can reach deeply into our hearts, in ways that far exceed the limitations imposed by the spoken word, there is a great deal at stake in the debates we have about it. The arguments usually divide between those who prefer contemporary praise music and those who prefer the traditional music. Sometimes the debate is inappropriately couched in terms of *spiritual* music or *good* music. The *praise* people claim that their style is more accessible and thus draws more people to church. The *traditionalists* counter that the little choruses have limitations that make God inaccessible. This response usually elicits the charge, "Elitist!" Back and forth the arguments go, like hand grenades tossed around inside the church sanctuary.

Church leaders who have decided to go one way or the other, or to try to blend their music, confidently assure themselves that their church has resolved this raging debate. But there are always members sitting in the pews who quietly despise the decisions that were made. If you are one of them, you feel lost and estranged every time the strange notes start to play.

Feeling Like a Fraud

You are not sure you believe anymore. Sometimes this uncertainty is precipitated by a crisis in life that wasn't resolved by God's intervention. You prayed unceasingly for help, but the help never came—and your worst fears were realized. So now you've started to wonder if there really is a God.

Maybe the crisis was intellectual in nature. We all live with a certain amount of doubt mixed in with our faith, but, in your case, doubt has overwhelmed your faith. Now you aren't at all sure you believe these words that you sing, hear, and pray in church. When you look at the faces of others in church, you can tell that they really buy into all of this. You don't feel disdain for them, just envy.

If you occupy a position of leadership in the church, you're afraid to be open with the truth. So you keep your doubts under wraps and just go through the motions for a while. But secrets can soon become dirty secrets that make you ashamed even to be in church, where everybody else appears to have found faith so easily.

Scorn

Perhaps you feel judged for something you've done, possibly for a breakup or failure in a relationship. You have already received more judgment from your own heart than you will ever be able to forgive. So you come to church, hoping for a little grace. The last thing you need is more judgment.

Whether or not a congregation really is judgmental is often beside the point. The church generally seems judgmental to people who feel contempt for themselves. For example, when couples in the church go through a divorce, it is almost impossible to keep them both attending worship services. It really matters very little how understanding and forgiving the church tries to be; it seems to be only a matter of time before at least one of the divorcing members wants to leave. Why? In part because it's hard to see one's ex-spouse sitting in church, and in part because someone going through a divorce often sits in the pews with the feeling that everyone is looking at him or her and thinking, *Shame, shame.*

It doesn't matter if people are really thinking it or not. You are. So you have serious doubts that you belong in the house of God, singing, "Holy, Holy, Holy."

Spiritual Loneliness

Underneath any reason for feeling like a stranger in your church home is often the deeper problem of spiritual loneliness. What you are missing is not just close fellowship with your friends but fellowship with the Spirit of Christ. You may deny this, explaining, "No, my relationship with Jesus is just fine. It's this church that I'm having problems with." But if the church is the body of Christ, then it exists as God's well where you are supposed to find living water. Still, as you attend the worship services, you sense neither spirit nor truth, merely the cadence of empty words falling on a barren desert. A problem with the church is invariably a spiritual problem.

Eventually this loneliness comes to all of us. If our thirst is for the water that only Jesus offers, then we must give up all other attachments for a while, including the church. Otherwise we are loving Christ only for his body.

The Reformers, such as Martin Luther and John Calvin, always distinguished between the *visible* and the *invisible* body of Christ. Our souls crave to experience communion with the invisible body of the risen Christ, who is sitting at the right hand of his Father. But the only body we see is the visible one, the church, which can never fully represent the essence of Christ. It is for this reason that we have also been granted the Holy Spirit, who binds us to the risen Christ. When we confuse the flawed, visible body with the invisible Christ, the Spirit will use even our loneliness to draw us back to the Christ for whom we yearn.

None of this is to imply that we should leave the church. Rather, it means that we must stay with the loneliness until the Spirit finds us. Ironically, it is often easiest to feel lonely within the bond of a community.

FINDING JESUS ON THE RUN

When people become spiritually lonely, most don't stay in their spiritual homes for very long. They try to run.

If they leave their church because they have lost their vision of Christ, rushing to another church down the street isn't going to help for long. Without realizing it, they may be about to participate in another church conflict that looks remarkably like the one they thought they had left behind. It is impossible to run away from the hurts that are attached to the heart. So the spiritually lonely are often drawn into conflict as a way of expressing the deep hurt they didn't even realize they were smuggling in to the new church.

Others leave and resolve to give up on church completely. Some will angrily denounce the whole enterprise, saying, "They're all just a bunch of hypocrites." But more often, church members are too depleted by their decision to leave, and they just don't have the energy to be that angry. They simply, quietly, stop trying. Like a lover who got badly hurt in a previous failed relationship, they are determined never to date again. But on Sunday mornings, when they sit alone at the kitchen table reading the newspaper, they catch themselves checking their watches, wondering if it might be time to get ready for church.

A few members of churches I have served chose not to leave physically, but emotionally. Never telling anyone about their struggle with the church, they just silently stopped participating in the programs and the fellowship of the church. The last place they wanted to be caught was in the after-worship coffee hour, so they quietly entered the sanctuary right after the service began and left immediately after it ended. Out of sheer discipline and commitment, they continued to show up at worship, but they had clearly left the church—at least, for a while.

Somewhere along the way in their solitary journey, those who are on the run will begin to do some serious talking with Jesus, just as a lonely, dis-graced woman did by the side of a Middle Eastern well so many years ago. The conversation may come after only a few weeks on the journey, or it may take twenty years, but it will come. When people who have reached this moment of sacred conversation describe it to me, they relate that the most remarkable thing about the experience is how unremarkable it was. There were no visions of blinding light, no booming voices, not even great theological discoveries. There was simply a prayerful conversation—and the certain knowledge that it was now time to return to one's life in the church.

So they come back—sometimes to the same congregation, but not always. Only now they are not a member of the church because of the benefits they gain or even because it is a place they enjoy, but because it is the place where Jesus has said they belong. They would never have known this had they not discovered that their spirits were wandering away for a time—a long enough time to realize that the invisible Christ alone has the living water they crave. Now, after finding this water on a journey they would rather not have taken, they follow Jesus back to a church they might still prefer not to call their own. Like the prodigal son, they turn and head for home, harboring no illusions about home having improved significantly while they were gone. Very likely the only changes that took place were in themselves. They lost their illusions of satisfying their thirst either inside the church or outside the church. So now they decide to bring their thirst for God back home.

We are told that when the prodigal son had spent everything, he came to himself.[1] We also come to ourselves when we realize, as are many in contemporary society, that the harder we run, the more lost we become. It is at this moment, and usually not before, that the memory of the father's house returns—and we decide to go back. We have no choice. It's home. It is where we have to be. We know this now, because we have come to ourselves, and we can't be ourselves away from home another day.

THE QUIET RETURN HOME

Jack Pembroke was a well-known cardiologist in a Midwestern community. An elder in his church, Jack had wonderful children, a comfortable life, and a bright career. Then one day his wife ran off with his pastor.

His colleagues and friends tried to be supportive, but no one really knew what to say to him. Jack was the strong, silent type, never at ease discussing his feelings. Still, he was clearly devastated. Jack had done everything right in life, but in the end he was betrayed by the two people he had trusted the most. It didn't help when he recalled that he had chaired the pastoral search committee that brought this pastor to the church.

Eight years later, I showed up at this church as the new, young pastor. I had heard about this terrible event during the interviewing process, so I was surprised when someone introduced me to Jack after the service one Sunday. He had stayed in the congregation.

Jack kept a lower profile than previously and never offered to fill a leadership position in the church again. But he almost never missed a worship service and even stuck around for the coffee hour. He was friendly, smiled easily, and clearly was involved in the life of the church.

When I saw him sitting in the pew, I would ask myself, "How in the world can he still be here?" We've had members leave the church because we put the flowers in the wrong place on Sunday mornings. Why did Jack stick with a church that had hurt him so badly?

It wasn't Jack's nature to talk much about himself, so I hesitated to ask him about his journey through all his hurt. But one afternoon, when I saw him making rounds in the hospital, I elicited a small conversation out of him. "Jack," I said. "I'm always so impressed when I see you in church—and I have to tell you, I find it pretty incredible. Didn't you ever get so angry that you wanted to leave?" There was a long pause while he looked at the ground. "I tried that," he said softly. "I didn't go back to the church for quite a while." As he spoke I waited for him to tell me about a cathartic breakthrough that had turned it around for him. But to my surprise all he said was, "But then I knew I had to go back to church." And he walked away.

That's it? That's all there was to it? It has taken me a long time to think through this brief conversation. I no longer think Jack was glossing over some deeper emotions. Why? Because in the long years following our conversation I have heard very similar sentiments voiced by others who have been hurt by the church. They don't come because it is easy, or even because they want to, but because they know in their souls that they have to. The way the story goes, the prodigal doesn't run home, but the father runs down the road to greet him. Frequently, the joy in the homecoming is the Father's, not ours.

No matter how angry or hurt you are, sooner or later Jesus will find you at the end of your spent anger or spent dreams. It's the moment you come to yourself, and it is at this same moment that you know you have no choice but to return home. The Samaritan woman made the very same discovery when Jesus revealed the depths of her thirst at the well. The very next action she took was to return immediately to the community that had hurt her so much. What else could she do? Now she finally knew who she was.

According to John, the crowds who followed Jesus eventually became so disappointed and confused by his teaching that most of them "no longer went about with him."[2] Seeing that the crowds had left him, Jesus turned to the disciples and asked if they wanted to leave as well. In one of his finer moments, Peter responded, "Lord, to whom can we go? You have the words of eternal life."[3] Peter didn't understand Jesus' words any better than the people who had just abandoned Jesus. But he knew he couldn't leave, because there was simply no place to go.

A COMMUNITY OF STRANGERS

Had the Samaritan woman not been so dis-graced from her community that she was forced to go to the well alone, none of the "respectable" people in town would have ever met Jesus. If finding grace means being found by Jesus, then it was actually the respectable folks who were truly dis-graced.

Nothing is more dangerous to the church than the tendency to define itself at its borders, keeping all the righteous folks inside and the strangers outside. It is so dangerous because by doing so the church misses out on fully knowing its Savior, who has always had a heart for the strangers, for lost people. He will find them on their solitary journeys and invite them home to the church, even if they are coming home for the first time. When lost people come, they do so as missionaries to a church that needs to encounter more of the Messiah than can typically be found behind its tightly constructed walls. As philosopher/mystic Simone Weil has written, "It is only to the prodigals that the memory of the Father's house returns."[4]

If the church is going to know more of the God for whom it thirsts, it has to learn from the "prodigal ministry" of those who don't necessarily look or feel like they belong there. The fellowship must include both elder brothers and prodigals—and even those who have no memory of the Father's house but who have simply wandered in because they finally started paying attention to their thirsty souls. If the church is going to be accessible to these thirsty souls, it dare not define itself by its boundaries. At times it might even seem unclear where the church stops and the world around it starts. Still, this confusion is no threat to the integrity of a church held together, not by its boundaries, but by its center—Jesus Christ. As long as we remain clear about this center, we can handle a good deal of ambiguity and diversity at the fuzzy boundaries.

None of us can be confident that we belong in the church. In reality, all of us are strangers to God's righteousness, strangers being drawn by the Spirit of God closer and closer into the center of the church, who is Jesus Christ our Lord.

This vision of the church makes room for people who look and act differently from each other but who are tired of being on the run as a result of their thirst for God. There is room in the church for the homeless who are just looking for a place to lie down, as well as for the powerful who want a place where they don't have to be in charge. There is room for the sinner who is looking for a place to tell the truth, as well as for the perfectionist who can never do enough. There is room for everyone who can make room for other strangers.

In Ursula Hegi's *Stones from the River*, a beautifully written novel, we are introduced to Trudi Montag. She was born as a "dwarf" in a small German town, and when we first meet her she is hanging from the doorframe, in the hopes that stretching will make her taller. The first half of the novel traces all the harsh experiences she has as a little girl who is different. Trudi is constantly ridiculed, as are the overweight children, the slow ones, the poor ones, and the unattractive ones. Trudi was one of the strangers in her community. But this alienation gave her a unique vision that none of the "pretty" children had. The author tells us often that Trudi had "old eyes"—the eyes of wisdom usually given only to people who have seen too much, which was exactly her experience as a child.

The second half of the novel describes Trudi's life as an adult. By then the Nazis have come to power and have initiated their awful campaign against the Jews. Trudi is horrified to watch the people in her small town, including people in her church, turn against the Jews, who had been their neighbors for generations. Some lashed out because they had lived with a lot of anger for a long time but hadn't known who to be angry at until the Nazis came along and offered a scapegoat. Others were fearful, and they contributed to the abuses against the Jews simply by being afraid to oppose the Nazi agenda. But Trudi chose to give Jewish people sanctuary in her basement. She knew what it felt like to be different.

As she huddled with these outcasts in her home, for the first time she was not alone. In this new community, filled with people who all had "old eyes," she discovered another vision for life. Listen to the way Hegi describes it:

> Trudi felt dizzy with the longing for peace, a longing as powerful as the passion with which she used to will her body to grow, as consuming as the passion that had fueled her revenge on the boys who humiliated her. And what

she wanted more than anything that moment was for all the differences between people to matter no more—differences in size and race and belief—differences that had become justification for destruction.[5]

Whether it is in the great sanctuary of a cathedral or in a crowded basement, authentic community is the place where differences are absorbed into a common thirst for another way of life. If it is God's community, created by the grace of his Son Jesus Christ, it extends to anyone who has "seen too much" and is tired of being on the run.

THE HOSPITAL YOU NEVER LEAVE

At the height of the Protestant Reformation a great debate broke out among the Reformers about the best model for the church. Some maintained that it should be a *school for saints*. Thus, these church leaders made sure that each of their prospective members was an articulate believer, a saint, so to speak, before he or she entered the church. The purpose of being in the church was to become better educated in the faith. Clearly, this is a church model that is alive and well in contemporary society. Martin Luther and John Calvin rejected this model and claimed instead that the church is a *hospital for sinners*. According to this view, every member of a church has come to this community for the same reason—to find healing for a sin-sick soul.

The strength of the hospital model is this: now the very things we felt we had to hide in order to fit into the school model have become the very invitations to enter community. No one has to be healthy enough in order to be welcome at the hospital. Our failures, sins, hurts, and other less-than-saintly traits are no longer reasons to be excluded from the community. These are now lost in the common confession that we are in church only because we *need* to be here, not because we *deserve* to be.

In Jesus' parable of the great banquet, all of the cream-of-the-crop persons who were on the invitation list failed to come. Therefore, the master of the house sent his servants out into the streets to invite anyone they could find to the feast, "both good and bad."[6] So none of us is at the banquet table of the Lord because we made the "A list." Good or bad, we're still never more than "Plan B."

Thus we enter the hospital-church to find healing from all the desperate mistakes we have made trying to satisfy our thirst with something other than Jesus' living water. Some may be further along in their healing and recovery, but no one is ever ready to leave the hospital. In part, the reason is because we just keep right on sinning and are always in need of a place where we can find gracious healing. Some churches respond to this "sin inclination" by trying to take away our innate thirst for something more. In their many programs and ministries, they advertise themselves as a "full-service" congregation, as if to imply that they can service your thirst so it won't bother you anymore. This is a grievous error.

The church's job and purpose is not to take away our thirst but to nurture it. That's the most important reason why we can never leave. Every Sunday we need to be reminded that we are thirsty and that nothing but Jesus' living water can satisfy us. Not even the church.

CHAPTER 4

WHEN PRAYER DRIES UP

A woman strokes the white hair of her beloved husband, who lies in a bed in the intensive care unit. It's not clear if he will live or die. The doctors say, "All we can do is watch and pray."

A young couple decides to have a child. It has taken them a long time to find the courage, but they finally make the big decision. Only they don't get pregnant. After a long series of fertility treatments, they find there is nothing else to try. Nothing else except more prayer.

A man drives home from a job he just hates. He has lost count of how many times he has asked God to get him out of this lousy job. Still, he prays.

PRAYER'S DEFINING MOMENT

Most everyone believes that prayer is a pretty good thing. Even those who question the appropriateness of prayer before congressional sessions or at school-sponsored events usually admit that prayer in and of itself is good. Thus, like most pastors, I am frequently asked to "give a little prayer" at a community event that is not the least bit religious. I used to chafe at these rent-a-reverend assignments, but I am learning to appreciate whatever it is that makes the public want to call out to God.

If someone tells you about a personal problem and you say, "I'll pray for you," the response is invariably the same: "Thank you." That's true even if the person is agnostic. No one is offended to receive prayer. Why would this be? Why do we all think prayer is a good thing?

The obvious answer is that we all know we are in trouble and are looking for help. Author Anne Lamott has written that she really has only two prayers, but she uses them all the time. The first prayer is, "Help me. Help me. Help me." The second is, "Thank you. Thank you. Thank you."[1] I like this, because I wonder if God sometimes gets weary of wading through all the profound theology in our prayers. However, the help we get from God may not be the help we asked for. God loves us too much for that. He loves us so much that he is determined to give us what we really need—namely, himself.

We have grown accustomed to hearing the testimonies of people who were in trouble and who tell us, "I prayed my knees off." After pleading for help, miraculously, in the darkest point of the struggle, they saw that God pulled through at the last possible moment and spoke a single word: "Yes!" Their prayers were answered.

Sometimes, but not as frequently, we encounter the stories of those who heard God say no to their petitions, and now they are thankful. "Today I can see it would have been a horrible mistake," someone testifies. "I'm so glad God said no."

These are indeed wonderful stories, but in my experience as a pastor, they do not describe the defining moments of a life. Rather, our lives are shaped more by the times when, in spite of all our prayers, God says nothing at all. We can handle God's clear no to our requests, and we can certainly handle the yes, but when all we get are bloody knuckles from pounding and pounding on God's door, well, that's when we discover what we are made of.

Sometimes, in spite of praying hard or praying well or praying often, nothing happens. Nada. Zilch. Not a thing. We didn't wrestle with God for understanding; we didn't struggle to accept his better plan for our lives. We simply talked to the ceiling—at least, that's how it felt. The prayer life that used to be a stream in the desert has dried up. We can stand in the cracked earth that remains and scream to heaven all we want, but there are no flowing waters to take us there. No one wants to stand up at testimony time and talk about this, but it happens all the time. As a colleague of mine observes, "I have found that ninety-five percent of the people will tell you that at some point their prayer life had dried up. The other five percent are lying."

When we have communication problems in our relationship with God, most of us are quick to shoulder the blame. We assume we must not be praying right. So we buy a book or ask the preacher to give a sermon on the topic. We try a few new techniques we've heard about from others. Thinking that maybe we've been talking too much in prayer, we try listening, hoping God will say something, anything. Still, the sacred manna never falls.

But we may not be doing anything wrong. When prayer becomes one more desert in our spiritual pilgrimage, it isn't necessarily an indictment of our faith, our discipline, or our love for God. It may be that we are simply being invited into a new, more intimate communion with God where words are simply not as important.

The Bible promises that the "fervent prayer of a righteous man availeth much."[2] We are not told we will receive what we want. Sometimes God's silence availeth more than his miracles. Mostly, what the silence makes available to us is a God who does not always come when beckoned.

We long to worship an uncontrollable Deity, but, ironically, when we find him, we keep trying to bring him under control with our many words. It is not until our effectiveness in prayer dries up that we will be ready to commune with this Sacred Mystery for whom our souls thirst. We never thirsted for prayer; we thirst for the God who is not contained by prayer.

PRAYER AS TECHNIQUE

One of the great arguments among the various church traditions is over how we should pray. Some emphasize thoughtful words carefully put together. Others teach the necessity of developing a "prayer language," by which they mean speaking in tongues. Still other traditions place great stress on praying in silent meditation. Much of the debate seems essentially the same as the Samaritan woman's claim that it was better to worship on Mount Gerizim than in Jerusalem.

Likewise, when I was a teenager, I was taught in our church's youth group that our prayers must follow a rigid formula. "*A*cknowledgment comes first," we were told. "Then move to *C*onfession, *T*hanksgiving, and finally *S*upplication." Always the same outline. When I asked why we were supposed to pray like that, I was told, "Because it's an acrostic for ACTS, which is the fifth book of the New Testament. See, it's the biblical way to pray." (It's a good thing they weren't using Ecclesiastes.)

By contrast, when the men and women of the Bible prayed, they dove headlong into their dust-and-grit struggles with God. They knew their struggles with life were rooted in a theological struggle with their Creator. Abraham bargained with God, trying to save Sodom and Gomorrah. Moses argued with God, hoping to convince God not to annihilate the people in the wilderness. When Jesus hung on the cross, he cried out, "My God, my God, why have you forsaken me?"[3] Jesus didn't bother trying to take the sting out of his words by encasing them in a lot of affirmation.

The biblical models of prayer beckon us to come to God to express our hearts as boldly as the patriarchs who struggled with God and as honestly and tenderly as Jesus called on his *Abba*, Father. The prayer techniques and languages we use do not matter nearly as much as the thirst for God that prayer must nurture within us.

Furthermore, although we are invited to bring boldly and honestly our many needs and concerns to God in prayer, the point of this invitation is not so that we can get a leash around God and drag him toward our dreams. Rather, it is so that we can drag our lives back into the hands of God. We cannot do this without being changed, since God's hands are creative. To pray is to change. As Sister Joan Chittister notes, "Change in attitudes and behaviors are a direct outcome of prayer. Anything else is more therapeutic massage than confrontation with God."[4]

Likewise, when we pray for others, we are also placing them into God's life-transforming hands, where they too will confront the necessity of change. So when someone says, "I'll pray for you," you may not want to be so polite in your response. Maybe a more realistic reply would be, "You're going to pray for me? Well, let me think about whether or not I'm ready for that."

It isn't that our prayers are powerful to bring about changes. They are no more powerful than we are. It is God who is powerful. We may not know God's will with respect to our requests, but we can be certain that he will use his power to change us, to transform us into a people who are extraordinary in their desire for him. If saying yes to our requests will get us there, then that is what he will say. If no will do the job better, then no amount of pleading will change God's mind. And if silence will help us realize that our ultimate thirst is for God and not for our requests, then we won't be able to pry words out of God's mouth.

CONFUSED BY PRAYER

When the early church was beginning to grow—and creating problems for the religious establishment in the process—there was a good deal of pressure on King Herod to do something to stop it. So he arrested James, the brother of John, and had him killed. Seeing how this delighted the people, Herod also arrested Peter. The church, politically powerless to do anything about it, gathered in the home of Mary, the mother of John Mark, and prayed for Peter's release.[5]

I have often wondered what exactly was going on in their minds as they prayed. Surely they had also prayed for James, but he had been killed anyway. Perhaps they thought that they weren't very good at prayer or that God wasn't interested in delivering their leaders. Whatever their thoughts, they certainly weren't prepared for what God did next.

While they were praying for Peter, God delivered him from jail. The first place Peter went was to Mary's home. When he knocked at the outer gate, a maid named Rhoda came to see who was there. She was so shocked to see Peter that she left him at the gate, ran back into the house, and interrupted the prayer meeting to tell everyone that Peter was outside. "You're out of your mind," they responded—and they went back to praying for his release.

It was easier for the church to pray than to believe that God would answer their prayers. I understand. At times I also pray as a spiritual discipline but doubt that anything will really change. I have seen "James" killed too many times in spite of my prayers. So why should God answer my prayers for "Peter" or anything else I'm concerned about?

Seven years ago I was diagnosed with an aggressive strain of cancer that had spread from my neck into my chest. At about the same time David, the twenty-nine-year-old son of one of my pastoral colleagues in our congregation, was diagnosed with colon cancer. We were treated in the same hospital by the same doctors. We even sat in the same waiting room together. Our loving congregation prayed without ceasing for both of us. Two years after my diagnosis it was hard to find any trace of the cancer in my body; yet three years later I officiated at David's funeral.

It was one of the hardest funerals I've ever performed, not only because I was so full of grief but also because I was so terribly confused. Even while I was conducting the service, my mind was being bombarded by questions. They came at me more quickly than I could bring to mind answers from my theological training. Did our prayers make any difference, or had God already decided to take David's life and spare mine? And for what possible reason? Or did God even have anything to do with this? If he did, then his decisions made no sense. If he didn't, what was the point in praying at all?

It is only a short step from questions such as these to beginning to think that our prayers are useless. Prayers don't change God's mind; they certainly don't coerce divine favors, and they don't even let us understand what God is doing. So during the days before and after David's funeral I prayed only because I was supposed to and because it was my job to lead the congregation in prayer, but not because I believed it was effective.

When we believe our prayer life has dried up, there is only one thing to do: Pray about it. There simply is no alternative but to remain in the desert places when we are led there, including waiting out the long dry spells when we are doing nothing but wandering around in the wilderness of our own prayers. There is no easy way out. It always feels as though we are wasting time in the wilderness, that we are heading nowhere and will never be able to leave. At no time is this more true than when we have entered a desert in our prayer life. But God brought us into this place for a reason—the same reason we are always led into the wilderness: to learn that our thirst is for a God we do not control.

So we pray our way through the desert journey. We pray about our confusion over the death of "James" or "David," about our anger, doubt, fear, and frustration—even about our inability to pray. We may wander through these prayers for years, not even sure that God has bothered to listen. But it doesn't matter. We aren't praying for his benefit, but for ours.

Chances are slim that God will ever break into these prayers and explain himself, but in time a day will come when we find that our concerns and confusion have evaporated. The struggles may not even have been resolved, but they are gone nonetheless. You will know when this day arrives, because the only thing that will remain is a thirst for God. To this day, I still can't answer any of the questions I had about David's death and my own survival. But the questions don't bother me as much as they used to. Somewhere along the way, as I trudged through the arid season of praying, I became more focused on longing for God than on understanding him.

"Dark Night of the Soul" Gratitude

John Calvin claimed that one reason we pray is to turn our complaining hearts into grateful hearts. Most of us recognize that we have much in life for which we can give thanks. We are thankful for loved ones, freedom, homes, work, and even the breath that fills our lungs. So when I lead the congregation in a prayer of thanksgiving, it can last a long time—there are just so many blessings in our lives. Giving thanks for our blessings is the first, and easiest, level of gratitude in prayer.

A second, deeper level of gratitude emerges when, in the face of great crisis or loss, we still manage to give thanks. For example, when I meet with a tearful, grieving family to discuss the funeral for the cherished family member who just died, the conversation often turns toward gratitude. The family is not grateful, of course, for the loss. They may be grateful that this person is now in heaven and that the pain of life is over. But they are always grateful that they at least knew and loved the person.

John Claypool, a prominent Episcopal pastor, used to call his congregation constantly to gratitude. Then his ten-year-old daughter died of leukemia. He wrote about his grief in a wonderful book called *Tracks of a Fellow Struggler*. The book portrays the depths of John's heartbreaking grief, but it also depicts his own difficult choice to be grateful.

> At least it makes things bearable when I remember that Laura Lou was a gift, pure and simple, something I neither earned, nor deserved, nor had a right to. And when I remember that the appropriate response to a gift, even when it is taken away, is gratitude, then I am better able to try and thank God that I was given her in the first place. . . . The way of gratitude does not alleviate pain, but it somehow puts some light around the darkness, and builds strength to begin to move on.[6]

This is heroic. It is a brave and incredible choice to be grateful, not for the loss, but for the gift, while we can hold it. But it is even more heroic to be grateful for God, who both gives and takes away.

This leads to the third, and deepest, level of gratitude to which the Bible invites us. Eventually in the journey with God an invitation comes to be thankful not just for the blessings of life, not just for God's provisions of both good and hard blessings, but now to be thankful for God alone.

The medieval Spanish mystic Saint John of the Cross wrote that in the life of anyone who is devoted to prayer there will come a "dark night of the soul" when everything is stripped away from you. Everything—even the blessings and the relationships for which you have been giving thanks, or the belief that you are making progress on the spiritual journey—will be gone. On this "dark night," you lose your instrumental view of God. He is no longer the provider of blessings.

We come to this dark night not because we have done something wrong, but because God invites us into the deepest spiritual experience of all—the discovery that he alone is enough. Not our experience of him. Not our blessings from him or our knowledge about him. Just him.

John of the Cross came to this night when he was imprisoned for the reforms he tried to bring to the medieval church. John Claypool came to the dark night when he buried his little girl. Jesus Christ came to this night in the Garden of Gethsemane when he prayed in solitary anguish. Sooner or later you too will get to this dark night. When you do, you will have to make eternal decisions about your soul. To what or to whom does your soul belong? To the things you are losing, or to the God who claims you as his own?

It is a terrifying night. You will think you're losing everything that is important to you. You are. All that will be left is God.

Praying Through the Dark Night

Not even Jesus received an answer every time he prayed. Just hours away from the unspeakable agony of the Cross he enters the Garden of Gethsemane knowing what lies ahead. Jesus has known it from the moment he identified with us sinners in his baptism. He has repeatedly warned his disciples that this day would come. But now that it is here, Jesus is "distressed and agitated . . . deeply grieved."[7] He is in such great anguish that he sweats blood.

Sometimes life's defining moments come not when our lives are interrupted by something unforeseen but when we finally must do what we have been dreading for a long time. We have prayed to get out of it, to escape this frightful thing, but to no avail. Perhaps you must confront an alcoholic who is destroying your family. Or you must let a daughter marry a man who looks for all the world like he's going to be bad for her. You tried to talk her out of it, and you even asked God to prevent it. But he didn't. Or maybe you have to move to another city—still another move you've tried to avoid. You can't believe you are going to "lose your life" again. When these unavoidable moments of crisis come, it feels as though you are going to a cross.

On the night before his death, Jesus took Peter, James, and John with him to a place of prayer. When you are about to face a cross, you don't want to be alone. No, you call on your friends to pray with you. But the passage makes it clear that Jesus eventually went on ahead to pray without them. It doesn't matter how many friends you have, on the dark nights when you must wrestle with something you cannot avoid, you know this is now between you and God.

Alone in the Garden, Jesus fell on his face and began to pray. "Abba, Father, for you all things are possible; remove this cup from me."[8] Can you imagine how this prayer must have broken the Father's heart? His only Son lay facedown on the ground, pleading, "Abba, Papa, please don't send me to the cross." But the Father said nothing.

God's heart breaks on all the dark nights we pray facedown in total humility. We have run out of strategies and plans and are now reduced to simply imploring, "Please don't let this marriage end in divorce." "Please deliver me from this disease that is sucking my life away."

Why would our *Abba*, Father ever let these prayers go unanswered? Why must we sometimes go to the cross, without any audible voice from heaven encouraging or even comforting us? Because it is there that we meet Jesus, our Savior, the One with the living water.

Our lives are not defined by the things we want or by the things we try to avoid. Our lives are defined, shaped, and molded by living in the hands of a Savior who finds us at the cross, where he also had to go. Finding us there, he raises us to a new life that far exceeds our expectations.

JOY IN THE MORNING

Ironically, the people who have survived this dark night are the most grateful of all. Why? Because the next morning they emerge from their fitful prayers as genuinely free people. They no longer worry about losing anything, for it is all gone already. Now their attachment is only to God.

Jeannie was a forty-year-old woman who came to see me after a difficult discussion with her doctor. Jeannie's cancer had advanced, and this last appointment had not been very encouraging. The chemotherapy wasn't working as well as they had hoped. Jeannie had done everything they had asked her to do in the great fight for her life, but now it seemed that her life was being reduced to the prevention of death. As Jeannie remarked,

"That's not the same thing as living." So she asked me what Jesus would tell her to do now.

I sat in the silence of the question for a while before softly saying that I thought Jesus would tell her to go ahead and die tonight. Get it over with. Die to your right to live. Die to your need to live. Give it back to God. By all means continue with chemotherapy, but cheat death by refusing to be afraid of it. Start your everlasting life today. It is the only way you'll be able to enjoy life on this earth—whether you live for another day or for fifty more years.

I recognize that I was asking a lot of her. But there weren't a lot of choices. The only real choice was in her response. The only way to respond with gratitude is to realize that the love of God is enough—enough, really, to change everything.

Gratitude—deep, third-level, "dark night of the soul" gratitude—proclaims that there is not one single thing in our lives that *has* to be there. It could all be gone tomorrow. If you doubt the truth of this, just listen to the stories of those who have lost a husband or wife, any semblance of good health, a nurturing relationship, or a magnificent dream.

Sooner or later we will all have our own stories to tell. We all lose everything ultimately—even life itself. And this reality confronts us with the greatest choice of all. We can choose to reduce our lives to clinging futilely to these blessings, and our constant companions will be anxiety and complaint as we watch the blessings slip away one by one. Or we can choose instead to give all these blessings back to God, and our constant companions will be joy and thanksgiving.

Many months after Jeannie and I had spoken, a couple, Jeff and Beth, came to see me for their final premarital counseling appointment. We had worked through the majority of our sessions on marriage, I thought, and we were now putting the final touches on the wedding ceremony, scheduled for a month later. But Jeff began this appointment by announcing, "I just have to get something off my chest. I'm terrified." He now had Beth's full and undivided attention.

Seeing tears flood Beth's eyes, Jeff rushed to say, "Oh, honey, I'm not afraid of being married to you. I'm afraid of losing you.

When my mother died, it took me years and years to recover, and I still miss her like crazy. I just can't stand the thought of losing you as well." Then he looked at me.

This was my clue to tell him what he wanted to hear. "What are you worried about?" I was supposed to say. "You're both young and healthy. You two have a long future in front of you. Nothing will happen." But I couldn't bring myself to say it. You see, Beth was about the same age as Jeannie, who was dying of cancer. So instead, I told Jeff that in my experience, one hundred percent of all marriages come to an end. Some end tragically because of divorce or, even worse, a premature death. But no marriage lasts forever.

Young couples often assume it is easier for elderly people to handle the death of a spouse. This is a false assumption. If the couple has worked hard at their marriage over the years, there is more love, there are more memories, there is more investment of the heart—and thus it is even more painful when the time comes for one of them to place the other into the arms of God.

This is the best possible scenario I could offer Jeff and Beth: to spend a long life together, constantly falling more deeply in love with each other—which will only make it harder at the end. Along the way, they can begin and end each day terrified that God will take away their lover.

I tried to explain this, then said, "So, Jeff, why do you want to go through all this pain and anxiety? I say, why don't you give Beth up now? Let her go. Don't pray to be married always, but pray for God to take Beth away from you today. Hold her then in open hands, giving up any right to cling to her. It is the only way your fear can be turned to gratitude for the gift of another day together."

"I'll think about it," he said.

As John of the Cross would have reminded me, I was asking too much. Only God can invite someone to pray with such complete abandonment. But I have seen enough of God's work in people's lives to know that, sooner or later, on some "dark night," Jeff will learn how to pray this most difficult of all prayers. My own prayer is that this experience comes soon for Jeff. It is the only way he will ever be able to enjoy his wife while he still has her.

PRAYING THROUGH SUCCESS

The dark night of the soul may be the most painful moment in our lives, but it is not the most dangerous. Our successes and achievements are far more deadly to our spiritual lives. This is particularly true when success comes on the heels of one's prayer.

According to Luke, there was a time when Jesus' popularity was at an all-time high. He had been healing the sick, preaching the good news, and driving out demons—and the crowd loved it. Every day the number of people who came to see and hear Jesus grew larger and larger. So it is striking that immediately after describing Jesus' great success, Luke tells us, *"But* he would withdraw to deserted places and pray."[9]

Most of us are pretty faithful about praying when things are not going well. But it is so much harder when we are successful. If a friend were to tell you, "I just landed my dream job," imagine responding, "Really? I'll pray for you." It sounds odd, but, as Jesus knew, it is during our moments of success that we most need prayer. Why? Because success is more dangerous to our spirituality than failure. When we're approved of by others, we don't spend as much time on our knees seeking God's approval. Nothing can dry up one's spirit more quickly.

Whenever I get together with a group of pastors, it is never long before we start telling stories. The first stories we recount are usually about the humorous and bizarre things that have happened to us in our parishes. Eventually though, someone breaks the ice, and we start telling the harder stories of how the ministry is going. There are always some in the group who are in a particularly difficult chapter in their lives. They may even weep as they describe the severity of the church conflicts, the heartbreaking deaths of beloved members, or the personal struggles at home. I've noticed that those who tell these stories almost always conclude by mentioning how much closer they have drawn to God through this dark night of the soul. Again, this is an example of the redemptive purpose that always accompanies the dark night. I have also noticed that those who have had years of success in growing congregations typically are the ones who ask for prayer. They say that it feels as though they simply aren't as close to God as they used to be. They also tend to have a hard time enjoying all of the success they see in their church—because parched souls are never satisfied by growing numbers.

In one of his letters to the Corinthian church, Paul uses himself as an example for all ministers: "We are not peddlers of God's word like so many; but in Christ we speak as persons of sincerity, as persons sent from God and standing in his presence."[10] The temptation to peddle God's word is great for various reasons: People want to have their needs met; it feels good to have the answer to their problems; it isn't hard to be a peddler. But it doesn't matter how successful we are as peddlers. It is only a matter of time before the people to whom we have been selling God's words grow weary of this effort. What people are really thirsting for is to stand in God's presence. Therefore, the first responsibility of ministers is to stand in this presence themselves, in order to then be "sent from God."

It is significant that Luke tells us Jesus withdrew to deserted places to pray. Where you pray is very important. To all appearances, it needs to be a place where you have deserted your success long enough to remember the truth—it's all a gift from God. Remembering this will make it easier to give back the success someday. As Jesus can tell you, the day when you must prayerfully give everything back is coming, and you will only survive it if you believe your thirst was always, and only, for God alone.

CHAPTER 5

COMPASSION FATIGUE

If your refrigerator is like most, it has become a gallery of things dear to your heart. The crayon drawing of a rainbow hangs a little crooked next to several school pictures. Just below the rainbow is the Christmas family photograph of close friends who live far away. You look at their wiggling two-year-old and smile when you read the words "Peace on Earth" printed below.

In the middle of all of these pictures of loved ones is a picture of the somber little girl from Africa you are supporting. Every time you open the refrigerator door to grab a bite, you remember the rickety shack she and her family live in. It doesn't even have food in it, much less a refrigerator. Below her photo is the smiling missionary couple who visited your church last year to raise money for their medical clinic in India.

Your love for your own family and friends easily spills over into compassion for those you don't even know. You can't believe how easily your heart breaks these days. Whenever there's a hurricane or earthquake, you usually dig deeper into your pocket to help the relief effort, because, well, you just have to do something. But you're already doing a lot.

In the mail today, you received a form letter from a friend's son who just graduated from college and is now hoping you will help make it possible for him to go on a short-term mission trip to Peru. You think you ought to help—he's such a sweet kid, and this would be a great experience for him. But the same batch of mail contained your quarterly financial statement from your church. The letter reminds you that you're falling behind on your tithe, and you still haven't filled out a pledge for the church's new building drive. You drop these letters on the kitchen counter, where they join yesterday's invitation to a fund-raising banquet for cancer research and an appeal by the PTA to help with the bake sale so the school can buy new band uniforms.

You have one child getting ready to go to college, another who needs braces, and a parent who must move to a nursing home. They're all counting on you. Sometimes it feels like the whole world is counting on you. And it's all because you're the kind of person who puts a child's drawing on the fridge.

WORN-OUT HEARTS

How many times have you heard a pastor or missionary tell you that the world is broken and it's your job as a follower of Jesus Christ to do something about it? The stories they tell are just overwhelming.

After hearing such stories, some leave church feeling depressed because they aren't doing enough. They feel as though they are letting down poor people, lost people, and God himself. They will try to find a little more money and a little more time to volunteer, but they know it will never be enough.

Others—these are the ones who scare me—leave church thinking, "God needs my help." This is actually heretical. Part of what it means to be God is that he doesn't need anyone's help. Undeterred by such theological fine points, these crusaders are filled with messianic illusions and are determined to "fulfill their mission for God," whatever it takes. When they meet resistance in pursuit of their goal, they only double their resolve to succeed. Soon they are hurting people in their effort to do something good. So now they are mean messiahs. They are like ambulance drivers speeding to the scene of an accident—and running over bystanders in the process. When it eventually becomes clear to the messiah wanna-bes that they are not succeeding, they burn out and give up completely on making a difference. At this point, they are more discouraged than those who never thought they had it in them to do much in the first place.

Sooner or later we all grow tired of trying to make a difference. We may believe that our lives are thirsting for a clear sense of mission, but mission tastes like salt: It just makes us all the more thirsty. Only when we realize this truth can our mission in life fulfill its true purpose, which was never to be the Savior, but to draw us back to him.

John Calvin learned this lesson the hard way. He first went to Geneva, Switzerland, in 1536 with a clear sense of what he needed to accomplish for the Protestant Reformation. Two years later he was run out of town as a miserable failure. Discouraged, he moved to Strasbourg, France, where he spent the most difficult years of his life. He had to sell many of his books and take on students just to pay the bills for his meager existence. While Calvin was there he came under the influence of Martin Bucer, who taught him a great deal about God's sovereignty. While Bucer certainly could have expressed these truths earlier, Calvin wasn't ready to listen to them until he had failed in the Geneva mission.

When Calvin first lived in Geneva, he began writing his best-known theological work, *Institutes of the Christian Religion*. This early edition, written in 1536, is not noted for its brilliance. But later editions of the work, which were written during and after Calvin's "period of exile," speak eloquently and systematically about God's absolute and total sovereignty over life. Calvin's *Institutes* is only two published volumes in length, but it became the foundational textbook for the next five hundred years of Reformed theology.

Calvin was invited to return to Geneva in 1541, where he led the Reformation until the day he died. In addition, his writings shaped and influenced the church in other parts of Europe, and even in the New World. Yet none of this could have happened without Calvin's early failure. The same story can be told about most every leader of the church throughout its history. They all endured at least one major failure early in their careers that changed them dramatically. Afterwards, these leaders invariably took themselves much less seriously and God's gracious compassion much more seriously.

This discovery is not limited to great reformers. It will come to everyone who is serious about trying to fulfill a mission. Nor is it limited to our sense of mission to the broken world around us. It is even more evident in our mission to the people we love and care about the most—our spouses, children, and parents. Because we love these family members so much, we try hard to help them. But what about when we fail them? This is when we learn about grace.

I suspect that every time the Samaritan woman stood at the altar to be married, she was convinced this time the marriage would be wonderful. This time she would throw herself completely into the marriage, love her husband, and make this relationship work. But five times she was wrong. Not one of the marriages worked out the way she had dreamed it would. Maybe they all ended in divorce; maybe some of the husbands died early. It didn't really matter as she stood before Jesus. What did matter was that she was exhausted from trying so hard to succeed in her relationships. She just didn't have it in her to try again.

So instead of risking more hurt from yet another failed commitment, she had chosen to live with a man who wasn't her husband. *At least the sexual intimacy will take away some of the loneliness late at night,* she might have been thinking. She was so very wrong about that. The physical intimacy would, in the end, only make her long for the spiritual intimacy known only in the covenant of being one flesh. But how could she give herself to another union, now that she had failed so many times?

How can any of us keep giving ourselves to other people or to other things in this world? Perhaps we haven't failed at marriage, but we have all certainly failed at something we thought was important. The more important it was, the harder we tried—and thus the harder it was to get over the hurt of failing. After doing this for a while, it's easy to become exhausted from caring.

So now we come to the point of understanding that our sense of mission won't relieve our parched souls, any more than prayer, or community, or right answers will. Like John Calvin, like the Samaritan woman, we are ready to talk seriously to Jesus about his living water.

JESUS IN THE PRESENT TENSE

Most of the mistakes we make in our commitments to compassion and mission are rooted in a far more serious mistake about Jesus, namely, thinking of him in the past tense. He was the One, we say, who was born of the Virgin Mary, lived a sinless life, and died on the cross. Since he atoned for our sins in his death, his cross is the bridge between our sins and heaven. All we have to do is believe, accept the offer of forgiveness, and cross over the cross to get to God. This is as far as we usually go when we describe Jesus.

I certainly wouldn't disagree with any of the above summary. But the Gospels clearly tell us more than that about Jesus. Most important, they inform us that he rose from the dead and ascended to the right hand of his Father, where he continues to intercede on our behalf. If Jesus is not dead, if he is more than the historical figure who went to the cross as the sacrificial lamb, then he is still the Savior—and we are not. So it is pointless for us to knock ourselves out trying to cross over the cross to get to God. Jesus is more than opportunity. He is the risen Savior who himself uses the cross to find us, lead us home to his Father, and refresh our dried-out souls with living water.

I find that most evangelical believers don't deny the resurrection; we just keep forgetting its significance. We will fight to our death for the affirmation that Jesus really did rise out of his tomb, but we often live as though his resurrection were merely a nice epilogue to a story that ended a long time ago. Now, we think, we must concern ourselves with the stories of our own struggles.

Why is it that so many of us who claim to be disciples of Jesus are always tired, while others (who are still getting so much work done) seem to experience so much joy? Could it be because the followers of Jesus who find joy in the mission recognize that they aren't the ones getting it done? They are simply beholding the salvation of Jesus, whom they are seeing at work in every part of their lives.

Unfortunately, too many of us remain fatigued in our compassion. When Meredith, for example, made an appointment to come and see me, I knew what we were going to talk about before she walked into the room. She was going to tell me she was doing too much and was feeling burned-out. It was a conversation she had had with me and the other pastors in our church before— often!

As if she were reading from a worn script, she began to recite the lines describing how much pressure she was under. She was overinvolved in the church, in her job, and in the community. She just had to cut back.

This was my cue to tell her, "Oh, Meredith, I'm so sorry. Please feel free to drop your commitments at the church. We'll find someone else." But this time I just couldn't do it. Instead, I told her it would be a great mistake to keep quitting things. I said this, not because we need her to teach Sunday school, which, frankly, we don't, but because quitting would have only added to her guilt. She felt like an exhausted runner, fretting over dropping the messianic baton she had never been given. If we in the church had kept encouraging her to drop things, it would only be a matter of time before she picked up another tiring commitment, which was exactly what had been happening. She was failing, again and again, in a game she never should have been playing in the first place, namely, the "playing Jesus" game. The challenge in life is not to do less, but to see the risen Jesus at work in every aspect of life.

The Gospel writer John introduces us to Jesus by stating, "All things came into being through him, and without him not one thing came into being."[1] Not one thing. Not even the things that Meredith was sure she had to get done.

The apostle Paul describes Jesus in similar terms: "In him all things in heaven and on earth were created. . . . in him all things hold together."[2] Consequently, *we* do not need to hold the world together, or our marriages, or even our own lives. We have not been abandoned to finish on our own the job Jesus started, for all of the work is still being done by him. "The one who began a good work among you," Paul wrote, "will bring it to completion by the day of Jesus Christ."[3]

As Meredith and I continued to explore the deeper roots of her fatigue, it became clear that she really didn't believe the Savior was at work in her life—or at the very least she was confused by his work. At one point she blurted out in total frustration, "I just want to know the rules. I'm really good at following rules." *Well, there it is,* I thought. Jesus didn't leave behind many rules, and the ones he did give us only draw us back to the need for a salvation only *he* can provide.

THE GOOD NEWS IN FAILURE

One day Jesus took Peter, James, and John and led them up the Mount of Transfiguration, leaving the other disciples behind. I've often wondered how these other nine men felt about being left out of this spiritual retreat. To make matters worse, while Jesus and the other three were on the mountain, the remaining disciples were failing in their attempts to cast a demon out of a man's son.[4] This was particularly troubling, since, according to Mark, Jesus had made it clear that it was the disciples' job to cast out demons.[5] *No wonder Jesus didn't want us with him,* they must have thought. Thus when Jesus returned from the mountain, he found these disciples engaged in a huge argument about their inability to get rid of the demon.

To this day, when Jesus' disciples argue with each other or with others, it is often because we feel powerless. We know what Jesus expects to take place, but we can't get the job done. Like Meredith, we simply don't know how to fulfill all of the responsibilities. "I'm just one person," we object. "Everyone is asking too much of me." We argue with the pastor, with our families, and with our supervisors at work. Most of all, we argue with God. "This is so hard. I'm not Peter or James or John. I'm just an ordinary disciple being asked to do the impossible."

When the demon-possessed boy's father saw Jesus, he ran to him and said, "I asked your disciples to cast it out, but they could not do so."[6] I know what these disciples must have felt like when they heard the father complain to Jesus. I too fail at the job of casting out evil on behalf of our children. According to a recent study, the number of unmarried teenagers who have become pregnant has doubled in the last two decades. The suicide rate among teenagers has tripled, as has the number of teens arrested for violent crimes.[7] We have already grown accustomed to seeing metal detectors in our inner-city schools—and the fact that we have gotten used to something like this is in itself evil. Teenagers in suburban schools talk about their own struggles with the demonic evils of materialism, racism, alcoholism, drug abuse, and—maybe the worst demon of all—loneliness. The parents in our churches, parents who know how hard the world can be on their kids, bring them to us at the church and ask, "Can't you do something about this?"

We try. Oh, we try so hard, but we cannot take away the reasons for fear. No matter what we do, the demons are still out there.

Like it was for the first disciples, this is when the arguing starts. First we argue about the youth director: "Pastor, this is some second-stringer you have. We need someone who knows what he's doing." Then we argue about the youth program, the budget, the van, and the facilities. But all the argument is really rooted in our fear and our intense feelings of powerlessness to fix the world for our children.

Of course, it isn't just our teenagers who are plagued by something mean and harsh in the world. Adults deal with it as well. Those of us ministering in Washington, D.C., find that there is no limit to pastoral opportunities here. When I mentioned this recently to a friend who lives in the Midwest, he responded, "Well, you aren't doing much good." He's right.

When I visit our mission partners in third-world countries, my limitations are even more obvious. I am overwhelmed by the poverty, desperate conditions, and political oppression. I do what I can, but it's so very little. When I leave, I suspect that our hosts who remain in the rubble and the slums rush to Jesus in prayer, saying, "I asked your disciples to cast out the demon, but they could not do so."

So I am not fixing things for the kids or the adults or the world as a whole. What am I going to do? Shall I call the elders together to say that I need to drop a few commitments, and start another argument about whether or not I'm the right man for this job? Well, I could, but that's not how the biblical script goes. It invites me simply to tell Jesus, myself, and those around me that I am not much of an exorcist. And it's just another reason why I'm so thirsty. I can't find satisfaction in my mission any more than I can find it in my personal life.

But this is, in reality, good news because now I'm ready for a Savior. The real question for every disciple of Jesus Christ is not, am I effective?—but, do I believe that Jesus Christ is effective? "I believe," said the demon-possessed boy's father. "Help my unbelief!"[8] Even this form of belief, mixed with doubt, is good enough for Jesus. So Jesus rebuked the demon, commanded it to come out, and helped the boy to his feet.

Here is the key to this whole narrative. Our calling is not to fix one single thing, but to bring all the broken things to Jesus Christ, who alone has the power to save our children and our society. But we can only do this if we believe and are convinced that Jesus is alive. And we can only believe that he is alive if we see him as more than a historical figure in the great drama of our salvation.

When we appreciate Jesus only for what he has done, we are saying, in effect, that in his life and death Jesus merely gave us a second chance at life and a list of instructions about how to get rid of the evil in us and in the world around us. Once we adopt this perspective, we become consumed with fulfilling these instructions and with not blowing our second chance. Thus, we keep talking about "my faith," "my walk," "my mission," and "my needs." But if we regard Christ as more than the holder of a set of instructions, indeed as One who is alive and at work in this world, then it is always his mission we are participating in.

We are never anything more than his witnesses. Both Old and New Testaments call us to be witnesses. It was the very last thing Jesus declared to us before he ascended into heaven and began his work as our great high priest.[9] But we seem to have become a little confused about the role of a witness in recent years. We've tended to make the term much more active than it should be, thinking it means that we have to convert people or induce changes in the world around us. Any courtroom judge will tell you that the last thing a witness should do is make things happen. No, all a witness does is tell what he or she has seen. Jesus Christ is the actor. He alone is the One who is at work today, bringing in a whole new kingdom. We just take the world to him, then watch and talk about what happens.

After Jesus had cast out the demon, the disciples asked him why they had been unable to cast it out. Jesus explained, "This kind can come out only through prayer."[10] Not through trying harder or learning more right answers or passing better legislation—only through prayer. Prayer invites us to see and recognize the activity of Christ in the world, even if our prayer is, "I believe; help my unbelief."

When we pray, we begin to see all of the quiet miracles that Jesus is creating. In prayer, heaven and earth meet—and that is always a miraculous event. When the church prays, it puts the world back into the hands of a risen Savior. What could you possibly plan that would be more effective than this?

HOLY EXPECTATION

Theologian Karl Barth once observed that to clasp the hands in prayer is the beginning of an uprising against the disorder of the world.[11] It seems to me that the disorder the church most needs to rise up against today is not our lack of morals or our secularity, but the despair that has led us into this long drift away from God.

I saw this despair up close during my regular interactions with a cashier. I almost always buy my gasoline at the same station at the same time during the week. Before the pumps were computerized to accept credit cards, I would give my money to the same attendant. The first time I met this attendant I absentmindedly asked, "How's it going?" Without looking at me he responded, "Lousy." It was clear he didn't want to talk about it, so I just smiled and gave him my money. The next week I asked the same question, and he again said, "Lousy." This went on for months. It became a despairing little liturgy we would repeat every week.

Then one day he startled me. As I was accustomed to doing, I asked, "How's it going?" braced for the usual response. But this time he smiled and exclaimed, "Great!" Astonished, I asked, "So, things are improving?" "Nah," he responded, "I'm lowering my expectations."

This is the gist of our culture's approach to dealing with hopelessness. Having been disappointed by friends, spouses, bosses, doctors, pastors—and everyone else we once expected to save us—we now think that the mark of maturity is simply to deal on our own with life as it is. Could it be because we live in a society that has disassembled all sacred expectations? Every day in a hundred different ways we get the message that life stinks and that the best we can do is to stop expecting more. No one has the answers, we are told. There is no salvation out there.

It is no wonder, then, that so many have adopted a variety of coping devices. Some cope by abusing alcohol in an effort to dull their disappointment. Others abuse their sexuality, hoping that bringing someone home for the night will help remove the loneliness. Still others work themselves into a daily fatigue so they'll be too tired at the end of the day to think about how sad they actually are. They just keep trudging up the hill every day to draw another pail of water, not realizing that their thirst is actually for living water.

Many of us who spend enormous chunks of time at church often do the same thing. We hustle off to Sunday school classes, worship services, youth group activities, committee meetings, and mission projects as though each is just one more thing to check off our lists. We become so consumed by church business that we do not recognize it for what it has become: one more addiction that serves only to mask our longing for something more, for something sacred, for something we fear deep down may not really exist.

Like the Samaritan woman, who only wanted Jesus to help her avoid her daily trip to the well, we settle for asking Jesus to help us cope with our busy routines. But Jesus will never help us cope with such low expectations for life.

As in no other time in recent history, the church today is called to stand in the midst of despair, trumpeting its scandalous claim that Jesus the Savior has defeated death and is alive and at work in the world. We dare not attempt to do his work for him, but we will commit ourselves to the sacred vocation of raising expectations for what he alone can, and will, do. It is clear that death and loss are never the final answers. There is something more: There is sacred hope.

Whether we are on our way to the soup kitchen or back to work for another day among those who are starving for something their materialistic lives can never offer, we must remember that we are never doing more than placing the despairing world back into the hands of the Savior. Then, and only then, can the miracles begin.

THE MISSION OF GRATITUDE

We may succeed for a while in taking care of despairing people, but eventually Jesus will make it unmistakably clear that he is the only Savior. The New Testament Gospels are filled with illustrations of this truth.

For example, at one point during Jesus' ministry the crowds following Jesus became so large and demanding that he and his disciples didn't even have a chance to eat. To get away for some needed rest, Jesus took his disciples on a retreat. They crossed to the other side of the Sea of Galilee, but just as they were about to settle into their time alone, they looked up and saw the large crowd—five thousand men, not to mention numerous women and children—heading their way. What happened next is absolutely fascinating: "When he looked up and saw a large crowd coming toward him, Jesus said to Philip, 'Where are we to buy bread for these people to eat?'"[12]

Put yourself in Philip's shoes for a moment. After day upon day of nonstop ministry with hurting, needy people, you finally have a little time alone with Jesus to talk about your own needs. Then all of a sudden five thousand people show up and Jesus, the miracle worker, looks at you and asks, "Now how are we going to feed all these people?"

Exasperated, Philip blurts out, "Jesus, don't you see? It's simply not in the budget! Even if we had an extra six months' wages, we still couldn't meet this need." Philip is very much in touch with his own limitations—"I can't help all these people." Meanwhile, Andrew takes inventory and announces, "There is a boy here who has five barley loaves and two fish" (which, by the way, I have always thought to be a huge lunch for one boy). Realizing how ridiculous his report is, Andrew's voice trails off as he says, "But what are they among so many people?"[13]

Anyone who takes the time to read the newspaper knows that there is a large crowd of needy people out there. There are crowds in violent countries who are being massacred, crowds in impoverished countries who are starving to death, crowds in affluent countries who are searching for something to fill the profound emptiness they feel. You put down the paper, only to find Jesus staring at you, his disciple, and asking you the same question he asked Philip: "What are you going to do about this?"

Every day I talk to someone in my congregation about a cancer that is getting worse, or about a heart that's breaking because of the death of a spouse, or about a life that's consumed with anger at an ex-spouse who is hurting the children, or about an addiction to alcohol or sex or work. I hear about the jobs people hate but cannot afford to leave; they need their job in order to support an accustomed lifestyle, which they really don't like all that well either. They come to see me morning, noon, and night. They write letters, call me on the phone, speak to me at the door after worship services, and ask me to rush over to the emergency room. They find five thousand ways to tell me how hungry they are. And after every one of them finishes talking, Jesus asks me, "What are you going to do about this?"

I respond in much the same way Philip did. "Jesus, I don't have anything terribly spectacular here. Just a lot of heart, a vague sense of calling, a few years of education, and some hard-earned experience. Jesus, I only have five loaves and two fish." It is enough. It is more than we need.

"Jesus then took the loaves, gave thanks, and distributed to those who were seated as much as they wanted. He did the same with the fish."[14] Did you catch it? Jesus took the five loaves and the two fish, and in front of the large crowd seated around him *gave thanks*. This is the most important phrase in the whole story. Jesus gave thanks for what he had, and then the miracle could begin. That is how powerful gratitude is!

I constantly remind my congregation that what distinguishes us in the world is not that we have happiness. Christians sometimes hate to admit it, but many non-Christians are happy. Nor is it that we are successful, for Jesus doesn't promise us that following him will bring worldly success. It isn't even that we have a sense of mission; I am continually amazed at how many non-Christians are devoted to doing good things. No, the thing that distinguishes anyone who follows Jesus is that our lives are merely an expression of gratitude for the grace we have received.

For too long we have indulged and distracted ourselves with complaints about what our parents, spouses, churches, and society have done to us. Hardly a single one of us thinks we have enough. Nearly all of us believe deep down that somebody somewhere is taking something away from us. "It's not fair!" we cry out. "I demand my rights!" Yet in the midst of the large, discontented, hungry crowd persists the image of Jesus holding up five loaves and two fish, giving thanks for what he has.

To this day there remains a debate among conservative and liberal scholars as to whether Jesus actually performed a miracle that day on a Galilean mountainside. Some suggest that Jesus' example merely taught the people to start sharing the food they had hidden in their cloaks. I believe Jesus literally performed a miracle. But frankly, for me it's relatively easy to believe this. The real question facing those of us who take mission seriously is not whether or not we believe that Jesus fed the five thousand so many years ago, but whether or not we believe he can do it again. Will Jesus use our limited resources—our five loaves and two fish—to feed the hungry, to heal the broken, and to bring hope to a world that never has enough of it?

It would take a miracle—but that is our Savior's worry. All you are asked to do is to take what you have, place it in Jesus' hands, and give thanks.

PART
2
THE LIVING WATER

CHAPTER 6

IT'S NOT ABOUT YOU

I don't remember when I first heard the phrase *It's not about you*, but I really like it A lot. I have yet to find a pastoral situation in which this phrase is not relevant.

When someone comes to me for the fiftieth time to talk about all the hurt caused by mean parents, after all the reflective listening and responsible counsel I can muster, eventually I have to lean forward in my chair and say, "Hey, it was not about you. They were too hurt themselves. You just happened to be in the way."

On those terrible nights at church when I'm stuck in a committee meeting that's going south in a hurry, it's usually because someone is too invested in a personal agenda. In those cases it doesn't do much good to keep talking about the issue on the table, because I know that's not what is driving the debate. I've found it's more helpful to look at the complainer and gently say, "You know, this really isn't about you."

The phrase is perfect for weddings as well. The bride and groom are standing in front of everyone, looking so much better than they are ever going to look again, getting so much attention and affirmation, receiving so many presents. Everyone even stands up when they walk in. So it's easy to think that this, at least, is about them. But it isn't, and their ability to maintain joy in their marriage is directly related to the day they discover that simple truth. Just look at their worn-out parents sitting in the first pew. They understand this.

Even when I sit beside the hospital beds of those who are dying, it is useful to tenderly remind them that even this most personal of all events in life is not really about them. It is about the God who created them, who sustained their life every step of their journey, and who is now choosing to call them home.

The real issue in life is always about God. Thus, the shorter catechism of the Westminster Confession teaches us to say, "Man's chief end is to glorify God, and to enjoy him forever." This beautiful insight can also be turned around to instruct us that the reason we are not enjoying God, or anything else for that matter, is because we have made *ourselves* the chief end. Life is not about our needs or complaints, our hard work or noteworthy achievements, our dreams or great longings. It isn't even about our spiritual longings. It's about the longing of the triune God to have fellowship with us.

FINDING FREEDOM FROM OURSELVES

Biblical faith has always made praising God its central goal, not because God is an egotist who needs lots of affirmation, but because the Bible is concerned that we enjoy the freedom that comes only from realizing it's not about me. If it is always about God, then we are relieved from the burden of pretending to be gods and can instead return to our created responsibility of receiving the grace that only God can give us.

Mark Williams was one of our church's pride and joys. For years he had been a junior high Sunday school teacher, adored by students and parents alike. Several people in the church, including me, observed his gifts for ministry and encouraged him to think about enrolling at seminary. He and his wife prayed about it for several years, then decided to give it a try.

I may have romanticized seminary just a bit. Clearly Mark thought so, for he found life there to be more than challenging. But, after days and nights of hard work, he made it. Of course, then came the battery of ordination exams and the struggle to find a position in a church. Finally, after all his hard work, came the beautiful evening worship service at which we would lay hands on him and confer the title *Pastor*. When I stood in the pulpit to offer the sermon that night, what should I say to this wonderful young man who had put so much effort into arriving at this profound moment? What else could I say but, "Mark, just remember, ministry is not about you."

As he sat there in his new pulpit robe listening to these words, Mark tilted his head a bit. He resembled Nipper, the RCA dog who thought perhaps he was hearing his deceased master's voice in the gramophone but wasn't quite sure. "Mark, ministry is not about your skills, your long hours, or your profound sermons. It's not even about your pastoral heart. What the members of your new congregation truly need will never be satisfied by you, and your longevity in this ministry has everything to do with you recognizing that. What your people are thirsting for is the living water only Jesus Christ can give them. Your job is never more than to be a guide in the desert."

No pastor could argue with these words. We know in our hearts they are accurate, but still they confuse us so much. *Surely, we think, we can do more than simply walk around in the desert with thirsty people.* Since the people in our congregations often expect us to be more than desert guides, it only heightens the pastors' confusion.

My hope is that Mark will stay in the ministry long enough for his confusion to turn into relief. But, like the rest of us who are called to practice pastoral care, Mark will probably first have to collapse under the burden of trying to be the Savior before this can really make sense. The day he realizes that it is Christ's mission, Christ's church, and Christ alone with whom his people must struggle, he will be free to enjoy the gift of not being Christ.

This same insight is critical to bringing up children, to caring for a spouse in marriage, or even to nurturing our own souls before God. It is never about what we do; it's always about receiving what God is doing.

Christmas is a wonderful illustration of this dynamic. I'm always amazed at how stressed members of our congregation become over this holiday. Even church activities go into overdrive during this period—which invariably adds to the stress. But have you ever noticed that children are never stressed by Christmas? They don't complain about all of the cards they have to send out, all the parties they have to attend, all the traveling they have to do, or all the presents they have to receive. Not once has a child come to see me during the holiday season to ask for prayer about his or her stressed-out little life.

The only worry children have about Christmas is whether or not they can possibly wait for it to arrive. Perhaps this is because only kids seem to understand the secret of Christmas: It isn't really about giving; it's about receiving.

According to the Gospels, the only person giving at Christmas is God. Everyone else is simply receiving this silent, holy miracle that breaks into the night. Much later a few wise men show up with gifts, but their giving is only as an act of worship in response to what God has given us.

Christmas is a poignant illustration of a dynamic we live with every day of our lives: We spend most of our lives trying to make things happen for ourselves and for people we love. But life is not reduced to what you give or know or achieve. Nor is it reduced to your mistakes, your failures, or your sin. Life isn't even defined by whom you love. Rather, it is defined by the God who loves you. In other words, you are not the central character—not even of your own life's story. This is not meant to demean you; it's meant to set you free.

FINDING THE CENTRAL CHARACTER

As Jesus continued his conversation with the woman at the well, he told her, "Go, call your husband and come back." When she explained that she had no husband, Jesus responded, "That's true. You've had five husbands, but you are correct, the one you have now is not your husband." A bit unnerved, the woman can only say, "Sir, I perceive that you are a prophet."[1]

Biblical commentators seem to be fascinated by this woman's love life, and they devote a good deal of ink to trying out various interpretations for the five husbands. The traditional interpretation is that this woman is simply bad at marriage and therefore stands in this account as a moral failure. Advocates of this position point to the fact that she apparently came to the well alone during the heat of the day, probably because the other women shunned her. What's more, she was living with a man to whom she was not married, and she later told the townspeople to come and meet someone who told her everything she had ever done, as if there were something to confess.

Recently, other commentators have speculated that the woman was a victim of a flawed system. According to levirate marriage traditions, if a woman's husband died, his kinsman would be expected to marry her and to raise a child with her. If this Samaritan woman had outlived her first five husbands, the sixth kinsman might have feared for his life if he married her, and might have provided her just a roof over her head but no marital standing. The advocates of this position point to the fact that Jesus makes no condemning judgments about the woman. Thus, they reason, she must not have done anything wrong in his eyes.

Allegorical interpreters, such as the early church theologian Origen, argued that the five husbands symbolize the five books of Moses (the Pentateuch), which was the only part of the Hebrew Bible that the Samaritans accepted as authoritative. Others note that the Hebrew word for *husband* can also be translated "lord" or "god." Thus, this woman with five husbands is a symbol of the whole Samaritan people, who were very syncretistic in their religion.

Yet another commentator suggests that the woman claimed to have no husband because she had matrimonial designs on Jesus. To this way of thinking the woman's response was something of a pickup line. A time comes for putting away the commentaries. When you run across an idea like this last one, it is clearly one of those times. There is no end to human speculation—and speculation is all this is.

Whenever a biblical text does not give an explanation, it is for a reason. It is as though the Gospel writer is saying here, "Don't waste time on what you are not being told. Don't become distracted by the things that are distracting this woman. Keep focused only on what you are being told." Clearly, the writer intends to make the point that Jesus knows this woman. He knows her history. He knows her great thirst for something more than what she has had in life. "Sir, I perceive that you are a prophet." This is our interpretive key. This is not a Scripture passage about the woman or you or me; neither is it a passage about all of the things we have done or are doing to distract us from realizing our thirst for God. This is a text about Jesus Christ.

Ultimately the gospel is not about our life's stories, our achievements, our sins, or our victimizations; it is about the saving activity of the Father, the Son, and the Holy Spirit. Everything necessary for accomplishing our salvation and our spirituality is brought to completion by the Trinitarian work of God.

Jesus was conceived by the Holy Spirit, and when the Son of God was identified with us in baptism, the Father ripped back the skies to say, "Yes! This is what I want. This makes me so pleased!" After descending on the Son like a dove, the Spirit led the Son into the wilderness, where he was tempted as we are. Through all of this the Spirit was drawing the Father's Son to us, even to the cross, where he died for our sins. Then the Son could at last draw us home to his Father.

When we encounter the story of Jesus, the first, and perhaps greatest, obstacle that keeps us from really understanding it is the notion that the story is about us. This may be, in fact, one of the reasons we have a hard time with worship, which at its best and truest is focused on the activity of the triune God.

So much of our week is dominated with a sense of self. Day after day we are confronted with our dreams, our needs, our sins, our problems, our work, our performance, and our health. When the traffic backs up, we wonder why they are doing this to us. When a teacher or boss negatively evaluates our work, we wonder how we could have been so misunderstood. When the family asks for more time, we tell them we just don't have any more to give.

Then at last we come to worship on Sunday morning, and we're confused to hear that it is *not* all about us. But isn't that actually good news? By the time I make it to church on Sunday I am sick and tired of me. I am tired of my thirst and tired of making the same mistakes over and over in my attempts to satisfy it. I am more than ready to hear a better story than the one that currently describes my life.

TRINITY SUNDAY

When pastors get together, they usually can't resist the urge to talk about the most difficult sermons they must preach. Some say it is the Easter sermon; others complain about stewardship sermons. But whenever someone mentions Trinity Sunday, almost everyone agrees, "Yeah, that's the hardest one." Not every church tradition designates a specific Sunday of the year to focus on the Trinity, but sooner or later every preacher must address the topic.

As one pastor struggled to explain this doctrine, someone in the front pew shouted out, "We don't understand what you're talking about." The pastor replied, "You're not supposed to understand; it's a mystery." Granted, the nature of one God existing in three persons may be a mystery, but we can still understand certain things about the Trinity. Here are some clear, and maybe even painful, truths the doctrine of the Trinity teaches us.

You Are Not Essential

In three persons, God existed in a perfect relationship before human life was created. We were not formed out of the dust of the earth because God was lonely and needed companionship. Before we were created, the triune God already enjoyed a divine community that was complete, lacking nothing. The true "holy family" in the Bible is not Mary, Joseph, and their baby; it is the Father, the Son, and the Holy Spirit. Or, as Augustine put it, the Lover, the Beloved, and the Love. Out of this sacred, loving family, everything necessary in the world has already been created. So let's be clear about this: All of our hard work really is not necessary to God. The triune God doesn't need our help raising children, keeping our office together, evangelizing the world, or resolving the great conflicts in our world.

Feeling better about yourself? You should, because there is no blessing in being essential. Things that are essential cannot be loved. Why? Because you *must* have them. There is no choice. And love is always and only a choice. It was not necessary for God to love you. The blessing is that he chose to love you. Moreover, nothing you do can induce God to love you more than he already does, because the source of this love is within the triune God, not you. God doesn't love you because you're cute, smart, or important. No, the source of God's love for you is found in the love shared by the Father, Son, and Spirit. Out of the eternal depths of this love God created human life.

Remember when you were a child, and you asked your parents where you came from? First your parents might have sweated a little, then they began their explanation by stating, "Well, Mommy and Daddy loved each other very much . . ." Then they went on to explain your birth. Humanly speaking, you were given life as a baby, not because you were essential (no one needs to stay up all night soothing a colicky baby), but because when parents are in love they become creative. Those children who are adopted experience an even more powerful demonstration of this. It wasn't necessary for your parents to choose you. They did it only because they loved you even before they met you.

In homes filled with love, parents continue to do all that is essential. They make great sacrifices simply because their child is a beloved son or daughter. So it is with you, the beloved son or daughter of God. In Jesus Christ, God has already made all the sacrifice necessary to save your parched soul.

You Are Adopted into the Holy Community of the Trinity

The task of the Holy Spirit is to adopt us into the Son's own relationship with the Father. Paul makes this point repeatedly in his letter to the Ephesians. In the first chapter alone Paul uses the phrase *in Christ* or its equivalent nine times in the first fourteen verses. Thus he teaches us that we have been blessed "in Christ with every spiritual blessing in the heavenly places."[2] We may not feel as though we have received every blessing, but this is only because we are too focused on our own stories. According to Paul, the Holy Spirit has also sealed us into Jesus' family relationship with his Father.[3] Thus, in being made a part of the true "holy family" of Father, Son, and Spirit, we have received all that heaven has to offer us—the inheritance of Jesus Christ.

This same adoption language is found throughout Paul's writings. "When we cry, 'Abba! Father!'" Paul claims, "it is that very Spirit bearing witness with our spirit that we are children of God, and if children, then heirs, heirs of God and joint heirs with Christ."[4]

This is the theological basis for our own spirituality. We must start, not with our own thirst for God, but with God's decision to enfold us into his family. In the words of theologian James

Torrance, "At the center of the New Testament stands not our religious experience, not our faith or repentance or decision, however important these are, but a unique relationship between Jesus and the Father."[5] Torrance, who is thoroughly evangelical in his theology, makes this declaration, not to discredit or devalue the importance of an individual's decision to receive the grace of God that offers a relationship, but to affirm that the gospel does not begin with any of our decisions.

Most people can remember the first time they said to someone, "I love you." It seemed like time stopped in that very moment. You waited for a response—and only one response would suffice. You had shown extreme vulnerability in uttering those words, and you hoped to hear in reply, "I love you, too." Through the work of the Son and the Spirit, the Father has taken the initiative to tell us that he loves us. The theological term for this initiative is *prevenient grace*. God's grace precedes and anticipates our faith in his love for us. We cannot even claim to love God apart from first discovering how much he loves us. He loves us as much as his own Son. He loves us as if we were his own daughters and sons, which we are—in Christ.

Beginning with God's love for us frees us from worrying so much about our love for God. There are days when even the greatest saints among us have a clearer sense of their thirst for God than of their love for God. But it really doesn't matter—as long as we are clear about God's love. We can always return to this love and rest in it, and in time we will find our own love for God restored again.

The Son Makes the Only Acceptable Response to the Father

Nevertheless, even when we become convinced of God's love for us, we struggle with the realization that we cannot find an adequate way to affirm our love for him. None of our right answers, fervent prayers, or obedient actions is without flaws. Thus, we can never be convinced that we love God enough.

As a pastor, I see many sincere members of my congregation knocking themselves out as they try to become acceptable to God. They sign up for Bible studies, covenant groups, church committees, mission trips, and seminary extension programs. They do all this, not because they think they can work their way into heaven, but simply because they are attempting to express gratitude for the passion of God demonstrated in the cross of Jesus Christ. But in their hearts they know that nothing they come up with is ever good enough. They are, in fact, quite right. It *is* never good enough.

Yet, we can take comfort that the Bible describes Jesus as both the Son of Man and the Son of God. Those of us who spend significant time in church tend to be clearer about Christ's divinity than about his humanity. However, as the Son of Man, Jesus Christ is the embodiment of our humanity. He was not a god in human disguise—which is how many people tend to think of him—but fully human. As the Son of God, Jesus was also fully divine—not half and half, but fully God and fully human.

As our representative of full humanity, Jesus alone lived a sinless life in which he demonstrated perfect, loving obedience to the Father. So it is only as we live *in Christ* that the Father hears the response of a perfect, "I love you too." As John Calvin explained in the *Institutes,* every part of our salvation is already complete in Christ by virtue of his obedience for us, and the Spirit's invitation to live our life in Christ.[6]

So, then, the challenge is to live in Christ, which is in the end only accomplished by means of the work of the Spirit in our lives. The Holy Spirit so engrafts us into the Son's relationship to the Father that our identity before God becomes that of a beloved son or daughter with whom God is also well pleased. As we open our lives to being *filled with the Spirit* (a phrase that occurs, by the way, in almost every chapter of Acts), we are transformed into the very image of Christ. I don't interpret this to mean that when God looks at us, he sees Jesus. Rather, I understand this to mean that we actually become more acceptable to God because we are being changed by the Spirit into the image of Jesus Christ, the beloved.

Paul told the believers at Rome, "Do not be conformed to this world, but be transformed by the renewing of your minds, so that you may discern what is the will of God—what is good and acceptable and perfect."[7] The Greek word *syschematizo* (translated as "conformed") is in the middle voice, which signifies something we do to ourselves. Through our own efforts we are able only to conform to the imperfect loves of the world. The Greek word *metamorphoo* (translated as "transformed") is in the passive voice, which signifies something that happens to us. As our minds are renewed by remembering God's love for us, the Spirit changes our lives. By God's grace, we start to look like God's will—good and acceptable and perfect. In other words, we start to look like Jesus Christ.

Adopted Children Have to Make Changes

While we cannot conform ourselves into being a people who deserve to be at home with the Father, we do find it irresistible to begin to make changes once we discover that, by grace, we have been brought home.

When I was a child, one day my father brought home a twelve-year-old boy named Roger. Roger's parents had both died of a drug overdose. As this family's pastor, my dad had done all he could to intervene, but to no avail. When it became clear to my parents that there was no one else who cared about this boy, they decided to raise him as one of their own sons. From the day he walked into the door, Roger became my joint heir in the family. He stayed with us until he had grown up and joined the army.

My parents did a wonderful thing in making Roger part of our family, but it created a lot of work for him. You can imagine that growing up in the home of heroin addicts was far different from what Roger discovered in the home of my pietistic parents. I can't count the number of times I heard my parents say, "No, no, Roger, that's not how we act here. You don't have to fight or scream or hurt others to get what you want. No, no, we expect you to act differently here."

With his parents constantly stoned, Roger had spent the first twelve years of his life consumed by fear, and, by necessity, completely self-absorbed. He even used to wonder if there would be enough food for him to eat. But now, in his new home, he had to learn about sharing things and demonstrating good manners and doing family chores.

Was any of Roger's hard work to change his behavior necessary in order to be part of the family? No, by the grace of my father, he had been made my brother from the day he arrived. But he still had a number of changes to make. It was only because he was so overwhelmed by my parents' love for him that he could make those changes.

Do we have a lot of work to do once the Holy Spirit grafts us into Christ's relationship to the Father? Are there major changes we have to make in the way we live our lives? Oh, yes, by all means. Not in order to be a son or daughter, but because by the grace of the Father we now are God's children. And when we revert back to our old addictions to sin, the Spirit reminds us, "No, no, that's not how you act in this family."

We will never make these changes by trying hard to get life right on our own. Only God's love is powerful enough to change our lives. He has so much love for us that we have been given every blessing in heaven. If we are still determined to pull heaven's blessings down by our own efforts, we will be constantly stressed and fatigued, and we will be filled with a spirit of complaining. We will never be satisfied, because we can't earn a blessing. But when we come to see what the triune God has done for us, then bringing about change in our lives is as easy as falling in love.

It was a terrible day when a telegram arrived announcing that Roger had been killed in an act of heroism in Vietnam. I remember my mother's tears most of all. She wept because of profound grief, to be sure, but also because she was so proud of him. He had given his life to save others. How could he have learned how to do this but through the sacrificial love of my parents?

Where can we learn how to give our lives to something other than the self-absorbed effort of trying to quench our own parched souls? Only in the home of the heavenly Father, who sacrificed his Son because he loves us and who brings us home through the ministry of the Holy Spirit.

Our Identity as Adopted Children Is Shaped at the Table

Most of the hard lessons Roger learned at our home took place around the family table. Time and time again I heard my parents teach him how to pass food, how to eat slowly, how to speak politely, and how to clean up afterwards. Through it all, they were teaching him how to live out his identity as a cherished son. If we are paying attention, we can learn the same things when we come to the Lord's Table for Communion.

One of the issues that continues to divide churches is their understanding of exactly what happens in Communion. Some refer to it as a sacrament, as one of the ways we experience God's grace. Others prefer to view it as a memorial or a symbol. Some emphasize the presence of Christ in the elements, while others insist that Christ was crucified only once for humanity's sins and is now at the right hand of the Father. But nearly all churches believe that Christ's followers are urged to come to this table, and all believe that something important happens in the process.

John Calvin claimed that what happens at the table is a "wonderful exchange." Christ takes our sins and exchanges them for his righteousness. As we feed on his broken body and his poured-out blood, we take in Jesus' life before the Father. It is for this reason that the Reformers always insisted that the miracle of "conversion" at the table is not that the elements change but that the communicants do. Furthermore, by the Spirit, who meets us at the table, we are lifted up to enjoy the great communion shared among the Trinity. We are given a place at this Holy Family's table. We cannot experience such communion without being changed.

For this reason, it is high time that our churches stop "celebrating" the Lord's Supper as a funeral. Often the church elders are dressed in black, looking very somber. The musicians play slow, reflective dirges, and the elements are hidden under a large white sheet (which certainly makes it look like there's a dead body under it). Before the elements are passed out the pastor says something like this: "Jesus died for your sins, so sit there and remember all the sins you've committed that put him on the cross." So we sit in the pews and think, "That's right. It's all my fault."

Are any of us really confused about our sins? I don't think so. What confuses us is how to find grace, and we don't find it by simply dwelling on our sins. By doing that, we have simply found yet another way to reduce the great gospel story to being all about us.

It is not about us. It is about what the triune God has done, is doing, and will continue to do. By the Holy Spirit, we are lifted up to participate in the Son's own relationship with the Father. All we do is receive. And that changes everything about our lives.

CHAPTER 7

THE SEARCHING GOD

It was the evening rush hour. The platform of the Washington, D.C., subway stop was jammed tightly with exhausted people decked out in rumpled gray and navy suits, clutching briefcases and bags containing more work than they could possibly complete in the night ahead. Everyone was lost in their own private thoughts. Some drifted back to the pressures of an office they had just left. Others fretted about stress at home, where they were about to return. No one was unaware of the people around them, but they didn't focus on them either.

On this evening, while waiting for the train, I couldn't help but notice a huge illuminated sign in the middle of the platform, looming just above people's down-turned heads. The sign portrayed beautiful young people with very white teeth, sitting at a table, laughing and holding on to each other.

It was such a strange contrast—all of us isolated, crowded individuals standing alone in a dimly lit station beneath a bright advertisement promising that, if we just tried this toothpaste, we too could have friends who would laugh with us. No one stared at the picture, but no one could miss it. For most people, it became a small, unnoticed memo in the back of their minds that asked, "Wouldn't it be wonderful to be a part of something like that?"

This is exactly what many of us think and feel when it comes to participating in the sacred fellowship of Father, Son, and Spirit. Perhaps there was a time when we felt the Father holding on to us, calling us his beloved as he did his own Son. But now we are more clear about our pervasive loneliness and alienation. We have somehow wandered outside of the picture into the gray, anonymous crowd—and we can't figure out how to get back inside.

FROM LONELINESS TO SOLITUDE

Most therapists and pastors will tell you that loneliness is the problem they deal with more than any other. It's not that people are literally alone in this world, for some of the loneliest people I know live in the city and suburbs surrounded by others. They have families and friends. They maintain busy schedules packed with appointments with other people. But late at night, when the busyness of the day is finished and they lie in bed, staring at the ceiling, the loneliness returns. It doesn't really matter if someone is in bed next to them, or if they drank heavily before going to bed. It doesn't even matter how many people they know. The loneliness will still break through when the distractions have subsided.

They toss and turn; they stare at the numbers on the alarm clock—and then they start to remember. They recall the advertisement that portrayed friends laughing together, and the young lovers they saw holding hands in the park. They remember the yearning for something more than what they have. Eventually their hearts feel as though they are about to break in half from holding so much sorrow. And they cry. Late-night tears are the worst kind of tears, for they leave us so lonely. No one sees them. No one is there to comfort or reassure.

Henri Nouwen, the now-deceased theologian of spirituality, wrote that we go through life with two great distractions. The *outer* distractions consist of work, television, phone calls, errands, parties, and all the other things we do to stay busy. But there are also *inner* distractions—the anxieties, bad memories, doubts, and deep hurts. Whenever we remove the outer distractions, the inner ones rush up from the corners of our minds; they can no longer stay buried. So as soon as we can we return to the outer distractions, for they act like a shield that protects us from the noises from within that scare us more than anything "out there." One of the greatest of these inner distractions is loneliness.[1]

The New Testament Gospels make it clear that, as a human being, Jesus also experienced acute loneliness. He knew the loneliness of being abandoned by the people who professed to love him but left him to die alone on the cross. He knew the loneliness of being a leader saddled with the responsibilities of making difficult and unpopular decisions. And he knew the loneliness of being completely misunderstood, even by his own family and his hand-picked disciples.

Jesus experienced the loneliness of being misunderstood immediately after giving a series of discourses regarding his identity. He had explained that he was the bread of life, the source of living water, and the light of the world.[2] In addition to all this teaching, Jesus had lived among the people, walked their roads, healed their sick, and fed their hungry. But even after all of this, the people still asked him, "Who are you?"[3]

It is a question also asked of us. The question reminds us that we are still strangers who are not understood. Or worse, perhaps we are understood but not wanted. "Who are *you?*" people ask. "Who are you to take on this new job?" "Who are you to ask me out on a date?" "Who are you to be a leader?" Jesus didn't respond to the question the way we would have. He didn't try to explain who he was by telling the people what he did for a living. He did not tell them what city he was from or show them pictures of his family. No, Jesus responded to the question by talking about his heavenly Father: "The one who sent me is with me; he has not left me alone."[4]

When the Gospels tell about the many times Jesus had good reason to feel loneliness, they show Jesus turning that loneliness into an experience of *solitude*. Sometimes Jesus physically left everyone to go to "a deserted place."[5] Other times, while battered by outer distractions, he descended into his heart to enter into solitude through prayer. What Jesus always discovered in solitude was that he was loved by the Father, who "has not left me alone."

Solitude is significantly different from loneliness. *Loneliness* is the unwanted aching of the heart. If we let it control us, it makes us needy and manipulative as we consume and use people in a vain effort to relieve the ache. By contrast, *solitude* is a courageous choice to set aside the distractions, the relationships, and the busyness in order to confront the heartache head-on. If we can stand to be prayerfully quiet long enough, we will discover what Jesus discovered. We will learn that we are not alone, but we are known and loved, even cherished, by our Father in heaven. Why? Because the Holy Spirit has adopted us into this same cherished relationship that reassured the Son in the midst of his times of trial.

In the middle of a lonely night King David once cried out to God, "You have kept count of my tossings; put my tears in your bottle."[6] David was not alone, and neither are you. God has not forgotten about your dark nights of restless sorrow. Only when you discover God in the darkest moments of life will you believe that he can and will make the sun finally rise and the new day dawn.

So instead of running from the loneliness, stay with it. Stare it straight in the eye, and turn it into a prayer of confession. It is the only way you will hear the word of the Lord: *I have not left you alone.* This is the only word able to calm the inner distractions of your heart, and until the heart is calm, all of your relationships will never be more than narcissistic outer distractions. No abundance of friends, no number of different marriages, no quantity of moves to new cities can ever take the loneliness away. The heart can only be satisfied by the One who created it. The yearning is for God.

To stand alone in the presence of God is to stand in a place of transformation. There our lonely hearts are re-formed and transformed with deep emotions such as joy, love, even compassion for those around us. In solitude with God we learn how to stop consuming people and to truly care for them. In solitude we learn to behold beauty and see the quiet miracles unfolding all around us. In solitude before God warriors are turned into poets, slaves and addicts are set free, wonderful visions of mission for life are discovered. For it is only in solitude that we discover the sufficiency of a God who also yearns for us—so much so that in Jesus Christ he came looking for us.

THE ARRIVAL OF THE EXTRAORDINARY

In reality, the thought that a holy, triune God has come looking for us is not particularly reassuring, because we are at the same time both attracted to and terrified by sacredness. Like moths to a flame, we are irresistibly drawn to the One who, we fear, will consume us when he finds us.

Holiness, by definition, refers to the One who is wholly other than us. God is everything we are not: pure, true, good, sovereign, eternal. Even to gaze upon God's glory is too much for mere mortals.[7] Thus the Old Testament describes people's terror during a theophany, when God appeared to them. They all echo a lament similar to Isaiah's: "Woe is me! I am lost, for I am a man of unclean lips, and I live among a people of unclean lips; yet my eyes have seen the King, the LORD of hosts!"[8] Woe is me! God has broken into my life.

Whenever we hear of God's arrival, instead of coming face-to-face with him, we tend to commit ourselves to acting spiritual. It's a lot safer than actually encountering the Spirit. Eventually, though, we discover that our dead-right theological answers, our estranged community, our dried-up prayers, and our futile mission projects haven't satisfied our dreaded longing to face God. They are all insufficient precisely because we made them ours. What was given to us as a means of worship we have manipulated into our own story with capital letters.

When we become tired of our own managed and controllable spirituality, we decide to let God take us—if only we can find him. Tragically, by the time we decide to face the consuming fire, we have wandered too far into our loneliness. No matter how desperately we search, we cannot find our way to the God who is near.

Somewhere around the midpoint of our lives, when we realize we are never going to find what the soul most craves, we resign ourselves merely to fulfilling the unremarkable requirements of life. At the end of an ordinary day at our ordinary jobs, we drive home to our ordinary homes. There the evening passes by, pretty much as we knew it would. We eat a meal, do the dishes, pay some bills, and fall asleep watching television. Then we go back to the same job the next morning. Or once again we shuttle the kids to

school and soccer practice. Along the way, we realize we have suc-
cumbed to our greatest fear in life: We are stuck with ourselves.

Then one day, as we are making just one more trip to the well,
we discover that God has come looking for us right where we are,
in the ordinary places. The Bible is clear on this. Because we are
never going to find our own way to the Sacred One who can satisfy our thirst and penetrate our loneliness, God has come to us.
He came like a shepherd looking for lost sheep, like a father running down the road to greet the prodigal, like a woman tearing her
house apart looking for a lost coin, like a man waiting at the well
with the offer of living water.

This is how the Bible introduces us to Jesus. He arrived as God
in the flesh, walking into the ordinary places of a world gone desperately wrong. Whenever Jesus met people he peered beneath
their ambitions, their sins, and their cloaks of righteousness.
Relentlessly he searched for the parched souls of both Jews and
Samaritans, and when he found them, he gave them living water
that gushes up to eternal life.

This gracious journey of the Father, who comes to us in the
Son, by the power of the Holy Spirit, has forever transformed the
spiritual agenda. No longer do we futilely have to try to climb our
way back up to heaven on our own. God has climbed down to us,
making our ordinary lives holy by his presence.

BEING AMAZED

Luke begins his Gospel by describing the terrifying amazement
produced by God's arrival in the flesh. Every time an angel came
with the announcement of the birth of John the Baptist or the
birth of Jesus Christ, the message was the same: *I have good news
for you from God.* And every time the human response was the same
as well: "When Zechariah saw him, he was terrified; and fear overwhelmed him."[9] Mary "was much perplexed by his words. . . . The
angel said to her, 'Do not be afraid, Mary.'"[10] Even the shepherds
living in the fields were terrified.

When Zechariah announced that his son, the one who would
prepare the way for God's Messiah, was to be named John, all who
heard him were amazed.[11] When the shepherds told others about
the angelic announcement concerning the birth of the Christ child,

all who heard it were amazed.[12] When the old man Simeon, who had spent his life waiting for the arrival of this child, prophesied that Jesus would bring salvation, Joseph and Mary were amazed.[13] Why was everyone so amazed by the events surrounding Jesus' birth? Because they had all grown accustomed to ordinary loneliness.

To be amazed is to be filled with wonder, awe, and even confusion. We think about nothing else when we are amazed. We are too overwhelmed, too lost in the presence of this thing that is so out of the ordinary, so unexpected and strange.

This sense of amazement seems to be an even stranger feeling to us than it was to those who gathered around the birth of Jesus. We live in a world that has crowded much of the amazement out of life. The people of that day, however, lived in a world that recognized angels and demons, a world with little or no border between the sacred and the secular. They were amazed virtually all of the time. By contrast, we live in an "enlightened" world of scientific explanations, recognized routines, and utter predictability. So it is not surprising that when we develop our spiritual routines, we manage them so closely and hold them so tightly that they have lost nearly all potential to amaze us.

Zechariah was an old priest. He and his wife Elizabeth had nearly everything they wanted in life. They scrupulously kept God's commands and were righteous in his eyes. Their only lament was that they had no child. You know they had to have spent years pleading with God. Still no child. Then one day it was determined by lot that Zechariah was to enter the sanctuary of the Lord to offer prayers and incense for the people. Again he was praying. No doubt Elizabeth was praying as well, and we are told that all the people were praying outside the sanctuary. Suddenly an angel interrupted Zechariah's prayers to announce that he and Elizabeth would indeed have a son. An amazed Zechariah could only say, "How will I know that this is so?"[14]

Like this old priest, we are more accustomed to speaking when we pray than to listening. What would it do to us if God suddenly interrupted our prayers to tell us he was granting us what we most wanted? I know exactly what it would do. It would amaze us and terrify us, and it would make us want to return to simply praying for what we want. We prefer asking over receiving, because we can control the act of asking. But when we receive, we become frightened mortals with unclean lips who are now in the presence of a holy and inscrutable God.

I was thirty-six years old when the pastoral nominating committee called and asked me to become the pastor of The National Presbyterian Church in Washington, D.C. The interview process had gone on for well over a year. During this time, not a single day went by that I did not pray over this decision. A day came when my wife and I were certain that this was what we wanted, but we were not at all convinced that the committee wanted us. The church had a rich history of long pastorates, with pastors who retired from this church. Even the interim pastor was more than twice my age, so the odds were clearly against someone as young and inexperienced as I. We kept on praying as the interviewing process continued, but I had convinced myself the position would go to another candidate.

When finally the call came and the committee chairperson said, "Craig, we would like to present you to the church as our candidate," all I could say was, "Me? How can this be?" It's not that I was modest; if truth be told, I was terrified. I had grown comfortable asking for this job; yet now that it had arrived, I could only fear I had received a call from God. Even then, I knew enough about God's call to recognize that God only asks us to do things that are way over our heads—so we can continue to be amazed by his deliverance.

HOLINESS ON THE LOOSE

All four Gospels begin their account of Jesus' ministry by describing the preparatory work of John the Baptist. People flocked to the Jordan River to hear John preach, then they would repent and be baptized. The purpose of John's baptism was to wash away the filth of sin so people could start over in their pursuit of holiness. It was similar to our modern prayers of confession. Since, however, people kept sinning after receiving John's baptism, they had to come back to be rebaptized and start over, trying yet again to get their lives in order. To motivate people to break this vicious cycle, John warned them that the Messiah was coming, and they needed to be prepared. When the Messiah arrived, he would rain down fire from heaven on anyone who was unrighteous.

Ironically, even though our society scoffs at this type of "turn-or-burn" preaching, it keeps giving us the same message. In our workplaces, in our schools, and perhaps even in our homes we constantly hear that it is up to us to get our lives right. We are evaluated and measured on the day we are born, and it doesn't stop until the day someone stands to read the eulogy at our funeral. When we fail at something important—losing a job or going through a divorce—it may very well feel like fire is raining down on our heads. So we're not particularly surprised to hear John warn us about God's judgment. Why shouldn't God judge us? Everyone else is criticizing us, so God might just as well take a number and get in line. No matter how hard we try, we can never get life right—certainly not right enough for God.

So we are just as confused as John the Baptist was the day the Son of God showed up in the wilderness and asked to be baptized. "What?" we ask along with John. "Jesus, you haven't failed. You are the standard we seek to meet, the judge we strive to satisfy. Why are *you* here to have sins washed away?" Jesus explained that his baptism was necessary "to fulfill all righteousness."[15] In other words, it's the only way we can be made right: Jesus, the sinless one, the perfect judge, must come to us, who are hopelessly lost in a sea of good intentions.

In that baptism, Jesus changed everything. Now we are made right with God, not by trying harder, but by recognizing that God is with us, forgiving us and causing us to be at home within the triune fellowship. As soon as Jesus was baptized, the heavens opened, a dove—a symbol of the Holy Spirit—descended, and the Father declared, "This is my Son, the Beloved, with whom I am well pleased."[16] The entire Trinity showed up on the day Jesus found us reeling from the impossible task of trying to clean up our lives; now there isn't much left for us to do but to receive God's grace.

So when God says, "You shall be holy, for I am holy,"[17] he is not giving us an imperative. He is making a promise. In Jesus Christ, we *shall* be holy. We do not become holy by trying to obey Jesus' teachings. Instead, we are made holy by allowing the Holy Spirit to draw us so close to Jesus that his love begins to flow through our veins, changing our hearts, renewing our minds, and making us holy in every aspect of life.

In order to understand the New Testament teaching about this, we must first return to the Old Testament Levitical law that called all Israelites to be holy in every aspect of their lives. Their relationships with family members, with the community, and with the king were all to be holy. They had holy days, holy clothes, holy utensils, holy washings, holy sacrifices, and holy food—the list goes on and on. Not one of these things was holy in itself, but they were all made holy as they were used to draw people to the Lord God, who was in their midst. The "dwelling place" of Yahweh was a sacred room called the "Holy of Holies" (the "most holy place"), which stood in the center of the tabernacle (and later in the temple), which was, in turn, in the center of the community.[18] Thus, all of life was made holy, through its center in the "Holy of Holies," where holiness resided.

In Jesus Christ, however, the holy meeting place of God has come to us. So we no longer huddle around a *picture* of community, like lonely commuters waiting for a train to take us home. In Christ, the community has broken out of the picture and come to us.

This is exactly the reality that was, and is, so confusing to people. No one understood Jesus when he declared that the people would destroy the temple but that he would raise it again in three days.[19] It never occurred to the people in the crowd, or even to his disciples, that he was talking about himself, because they just couldn't imagine that Jesus was the new meeting place for a holy God and a sinful people. But the moment Jesus took his last breath on the cross, the curtain in the temple that separated the holiness of God from the rest of the world was torn in two, from top to bottom, and the holiness rushed out of that room into every crevice of the world, wherever the Holy Spirit took it.

Expounding on the great significance of this, Paul claimed that for those who are in Christ, all food is now clean, all days are holy, all places are sacred.[20] All work done in the name of Jesus is now our work as members of the "holy priesthood," whose function is to offer spiritual sacrifices of gratitude to God for what he has done for us in Christ.[21] In Christ, there is no longer a veiled distinction between sacred and secular. When, by the Holy Spirit, we see the risen Jesus in our midst, it's all sacred.

THE TWO HANDS OF GOD

One of the earliest heresies the church struggled with was Gnosticism, which invited people to ascend to God through private, even secret, "knowledge" (Greek, *gnosis*). Among other things, this heresy led people to abandon interest in the physical body or the fallen material world, as they individually climbed closer and closer to God. Not surprisingly, Gnostics rejected the Incarnation, claiming that God would never become flesh. They also rejected the doctrine of the bodily resurrection, preferring instead to say that in death the spirit is released from the "prison-house" of the body. For the Gnostics, Jesus was not *God with us* in the flesh, but the exemplar of a perfectionism that is possible for all who follow his pattern of spiritual ascent.

We still see the legacy of the Gnostics, now disguised as "spirituality," in the teaching that invites us individually to ascend to God through knowledge and renunciation of a world that we are merely passing through.[22] The church has always called such teaching heresy because, as was evident in Jesus' baptism, hope is found only through the descent of God in Word and Spirit.

The early church father Irenaeus challenged the Gnostics as he wrote about the two hands of God. One of these hands is Jesus Christ, the Word of God made flesh, who descends into our midst and makes life holy by his presence. The other is the Spirit of God, who lifts us up and engrafts us into the risen Christ. God the Father uses both of these hands, Irenaeus said, to embrace us—this is the ministry of the blessed Trinity. Like the prodigal son's father who wraps both hands around him, embracing him, kissing him, rejoicing that the lost is found, so God takes us in both arms. This isn't some wimpy, one-arm, side-by-side embrace. The Son and the Spirit become God's two-handed embrace, drawing all of life into the heart of his holiness.

Salvation means that when God finds us, he receives all that there is. He rejects nothing—not our ordinary routines, not even our great regrets. When we offer to God our grave mistakes and the grievous sins of our past, we discover that there is a holy use for everything. In God's hands, life is no longer a challenge we need to get right, but a holy gift to be received with awe, reverence, and faithfulness. Now even the simplest and most ordinary work, if done to the glory of God, is an opportunity to hear the seraphs singing, "Holy, Holy, Holy is the LORD of hosts; the whole earth is full of his glory"²³—including your own little corner of the earth.

Last year our church buried Kaye Stinson, a young mother, a devoted wife, and a lover of Jesus Christ. One day I had gone to visit Kaye in her home for what we both knew would be the last time I would see her alive. We talked, prayed, and read and discussed various Scriptures. I reassured Kaye about our church's commitment to care for her family. We planned her funeral, selecting all the texts and hymns, and we cried. But we both knew we were not alone in the room. It became the "Holy of Holies" because the Spirit was there, preparing to bring Kaye home.

After Kaye and I said good-bye, her husband John led me outside to the porch of their home, where we talked a bit. Suddenly their eight-year-old daughter Elizabeth came racing up the sidewalk. She was covered from head to toe in mud. If it hadn't been for her ear-to-ear grin I wouldn't have recognized her. "What happened to you?" her father asked. "Me and my friends went mudsliding today," she explained. It was yet another holy moment.

Elizabeth knew her mother was dying. Her little heart was breaking with grief. But sometimes, when you see a muddy hill, you simply have to slide down it for the sheer joy it brings. You have to choose life—even in the midst of grief. Life is a precious gift that doesn't last long, so it's good to savor every holy inch of it.

Elizabeth would have made a terrible Gnostic. But she makes a great witness to our belief that God descends to us and, because he does, has made all of life holy by his presence.

RECOGNIZING YOUR MOMENT WITH GOD

Most of us want to believe that the stories of our lives will have a happy ending. We'll make better choices. We'll get out of debt and even save some money. We'll work hard to earn the promotion at work and even get serious about taking care of our health. All these expectations are born out of the nagging and lonely fear that we are on our own in the mission of improving our lives. We recognize we need a plan, so we count on a new deal at work, a new relationship, or a new diet for help. Like the people who lined the path leading into Jerusalem on Palm Sunday, some of us even count on Jesus.

As Luke tells the story, when Jesus finally entered Jerusalem on the back of a donkey, he became the star of a parade. Excited about all the powerful things Jesus had been doing, a multitude of disciples began to cry out, "Blessed is the king who comes in the name of the Lord!"[24]

Whatever we are counting on is our king. As generations have done for centuries, we will give this king an enormous amount of power. We will praise it to the skies, as long as it fulfills our expectations. But once the king disappoints us—well, we have demonstrated our ability to discard the kings of our own making, Jesus included.

As he approached Jerusalem Jesus wasn't smiling and waving to the crowds, as you're supposed to do if you are the grand marshal of a parade. Instead, he began to weep. Jesus wept because he knew Judas would become disappointed in him and betray him, Peter would become disappointed and deny he even knew Jesus, and the same crowd that danced before their king today would soon cry out in utter disappointment for the release of the murderer Barabbas instead of their innocent and humble Savior.

We know something about disappointment with Jesus too, don't we? We often become disappointed when he doesn't come to help us with our goals and our own carefully concocted plans for saving ourselves. But Jesus has come in the power of the Holy Spirit to bring us home to the Father. This is what it means to call him Savior, and the things from which we most need to be saved are our expectations.

Luke tells us the Pharisees in the crowd urged Jesus, "Teacher [notice they don't say, "King"], order your disciples to stop."[25] It was as though they were saying, "Jesus, we all know how this story will end. Why are you letting the charade continue? Don't raise the people's expectations." But Jesus replied, "I tell you, if these were silent, the stones would shout out."[26] The entire world, even the elements of nature itself, longs for the hopeful presence of God with us. Unfortunately, we often confuse hope with expectations. Our expectations are rooted in those things we count on happening. Yet, our hope, according to the Bible, is rooted in Jesus Christ—no matter what happens.

We are told that Jesus cried for Jerusalem because it "did not recognize the moment of your visitation from God."[27] Every life is graced by sacred moments of visitation from God. The question is, do we recognize them? Sometimes these moments are the wonderful glimpses of heaven we get, when, for example, we are sitting at a dinner table with people we love and the evening air is filled with laughter and deep, radiant joy. But often the sacred moments are not exactly what we were expecting. Often they look a lot like disappointment.

Sacred moments come not just in the parades; they are not limited to the high moments when we are carrying Jesus into our dreams. Frequently they follow right on the heels of the highs, when it is just another ordinary day in Jerusalem and the mighty deeds of power have dried up. It can be a sacred moment when you discover that your health is gone and isn't coming back, when you have just buried a loved one, or when your relationships are in the midst of a long dry spell. The disappointment of these moments confronts you with an awesome choice: You can look for another king, or you can say, "A cross isn't exactly what I had in mind, Jesus, but I will follow you anywhere. You are my only hope." Choose carefully, for this experience of disappointment is your moment of visitation from God.

Jesus' entry into Jerusalem was a moment filled with fragile possibility. Oh, what might have been if only the people had realized that this was their moment of visitation from God. "Oh, what might have been." How many times haven't I heard people utter these very words as they look back on their lives. They missed their moment. They were too committed to their goals for the way things were supposed to turn out. They didn't see the interruptions of life as an invitation to a new life. Now all that remains is regret. Now it is too late; the moment has come and gone. Sadly, it turns out that in the end they never had hope; they just had expectations.

We are living in a society that has far too many expectations and not nearly enough hope. We expect to get what we deserve; we expect to be heard and to have our complaints remedied—but we have no great hopes as a people. When a society loses its great hopes, the people in it live as if they can squander today, because there are no better days ahead. Economists tell us we're doing this with our consumer debt; sociologists tell us we're doing this with our families. We are squandering these holy gifts. Ecologists tell us that the earth is now in such trouble that even the stones are crying out. We need to have hope that something, or Someone, is coming down the road for us, or else we will never make it to tomorrow.

The hope supplied in and through Jesus Christ is not easy to contain, and it is certainly not what we expected. He frequently surprises us and, yes, sometimes disappoints us, but only his hope can lead us out of the darkness of our self-preoccupation and into the glorious light of God's kingdom. It's the only place where our lonely, parched souls can at last find the well of living water that gushes up to eternal life, and be found by the God who tirelessly searches for us. But the gate to God's kingdom is so narrow that you can't fit through unless you drop all your expectations—and maybe the briefcase that has too much work in it.

CHAPTER

8

COMMUNING WITH GOD

The bewildered, dazed disciples on the Mount of Olives just kept staring up into the sky, looking for a trace of their Savior.[1] When Jesus had brought them there, they must have remembered that they had been there with him just before he entered Jerusalem on Palm Sunday—the time when they first thought he was going in to take charge of the kingdom of Israel. Of course, that's not how things turned out. When Jesus was crucified, they were crushed. When he rose from the dead, they were shocked. We are not told what they were feeling during the next forty days, as the risen Jesus talked to them about the kingdom of God. Maybe they were too numb to have feelings any longer.

Finding themselves with Jesus back on the Mount of Olives, it was only logical for the disciples to hope that maybe now, finally, they were going to take Jerusalem by storm: "Lord, is this the time when you will restore the kingdom to Israel?"[2] But Jesus didn't ride victoriously back into town. Instead, he first made a remark about receiving the power of the Holy Spirit to be his witnesses to the ends of the earth—and then he ascended on a cloud right up into heaven.

Not knowing what else to do and ready for just about anything, they just kept gazing into the sky. Then two men in white robes suddenly appeared beside them and told them to knock it off. Remembering Jesus' instructions to wait in Jerusalem for the baptism of the Holy Spirit, the disciples returned to the Upper Room, where they devoted themselves to prayer—and waiting.

HURRY UP AND WAIT

We hate waiting. Just because we get a lot of practice at it doesn't mean we're good at it. We wait in airports, post offices, motor vehicle offices, restaurants, banks, hospitals, and doctors' offices. It all leaves us just a bit cranky. (I have a recurring dream that I'm in hell, but it's actually the checkout lane at the grocery store. In my dream, for all of eternity I just keep switching to a different lane, only to discover that I picked a slower one.)

As a child I couldn't stand it when my parents would respond to one of my requests by declaring, "I don't know, honey, we'll have to wait and see." Like most kids, I could never quite grasp the meaning of "wait and see." I assumed it meant I had to keep asking for what I wanted. As an adult I've discovered that a good deal of life is spent waiting to see what will happen.

After a long surgery the doctor enters the waiting room and says, "We did the best we could. Now we'll have to wait and see." Or the job interview went pretty well, but you still don't know if you got the job. You must wait and see. In our congregation there are couples waiting to see if they will get pregnant, depressed people waiting to see if they will ever climb out of the dark hole, lonely people waiting to see if someone will love them, parents waiting to see how their children will turn out once they reach young adulthood.

We can keep asking our families, friends, and neighbors for the things we want. We can even ask God in prayer. But still we must wait and see. It seems that every important thing in life comes only after a period of waiting. So it shouldn't surprise us in the least that when we turn to Luke's opening paragraphs that describe the activities of the Spirit-filled apostles, the first thing we find them doing is waiting.

Acts is the second volume of Luke's history account. Both books are addressed to a man named Theophilus, and both are, at their core, about Jesus. The first volume, the Gospel according to Luke, recounts Jesus' teachings and the events of his life, death, and resurrection. The second, the book of Acts, still deals with Jesus, only now Luke depicts the *risen* Jesus, who is seated at the right hand of the Father and who brings salvation to all the earth through the power of the Holy Spirit.

We essentially know nothing about Theophilus. He could be anyone, perhaps someone just like you. Like Theophilus, you may have digested the Gospel account about Jesus. You know all the details of Jesus' birth, teachings, miracles, cross, and resurrection. Yet you wonder, "Why am I still waiting for something to satisfy my thirst?"

Luke's first answer to this question is that the Holy Spirit is the One we are waiting for. We may have thought we were waiting for healing, for a job, or for a fresh outpouring of hope. But Jesus makes it clear that what all his followers really need is the power of the Spirit. Among Jesus' concluding words in Luke's Gospel are these: "I am sending upon you what my Father promised; so stay here in the city until you have been clothed with power from on high."[3] The book of Acts begins with Jesus promising yet again that we will be baptized with this Spirit.

It wasn't until Acts 2, at the event called Pentecost, that this baptism of the Holy Spirit occurred. The disciples' prayerful waiting was interrupted by a deafening sound like the rush of a mighty wind. What looked like divided tongues of fire appeared over the heads of the disciples, and "all of them were filled with the Holy Spirit and began to speak in other languages, as the Spirit gave them ability."[4] This is not a calm, controlled scene. The house in which they were meeting was torn apart by the arrival of the Spirit, who pushed the waiting disciples out into the world. Jesus' disciples could never again be the same. They were transformed from being the often timid, confused, uneducated disciples portrayed in Luke's Gospel to being the bold and visionary apostles who turned the world upside down.

Jesus would pour the same Spirit into our lives today. In the power of the Spirit, the same marvelous things begin to happen to us. Loneliness is turned into the rich fellowship of prayer. Marriage is turned into the joy of mutual submission. Sickness is turned into a mere thorn in the flesh. Jobs are turned into mission. "Living is Christ and dying is gain," as the Holy Spirit engrafts our lives into Christ's unfolding drama of salvation in the world.[5]

So why all the waiting? If this drama is so wonderful, why doesn't the story of Acts begin in chapter 1 with Pentecost and the coming of the Spirit? Why do we still have this deep, insatiable thirst of the soul after so many years, after so many spiritual retreats where we seek the face of the Lord?

The waiting isn't wasted time. In fact, it's one of the most critical chapters of the story. Waiting reminds us that we are not powerful enough to make things happen, which is, of course, why we're waiting. We're not even able to quench our own spiritual thirst. When we finally recognize this limitation, our true self emerges from beneath the happy veneer. In short, how we wait tells God a lot about us.

After Ernest Hemingway was wounded during World War I, the medical staff pulled 237 pieces of shrapnel out of his body. It was a formative experience for him as he waited through the long period of convalescence. During that time he observed that some of his fellow hospital patients were strengthened by this long sojourn through the stressful waiting, while others were shown to be shallow and immature. In every case the waiting brought out the true nature of the person.

From this experience Hemingway developed the basic story line for his novels. He would put seemingly "good" people into difficult situations in which they were forced to wait—through times of combat, in anticipation of deadly bulls, or during long, despairing days adrift at sea. Hemingway's thesis was that these scenes would enable us to see what people are really made of. The waiting does not break people, he claimed, but instead reveals them.

In reality, this is precisely what waiting does—it reveals character. In order to be in tune with Jesus' mission in the world, we must be men and women of spiritual character. So during the waiting period we may find ourselves in, God has chosen also to wait and see, to discover what we are made of. Is he going to see cranky impatience? Or will he see a deep, confident peacefulness focused on settling for nothing less than the living water of the Holy Spirit?

THE LIVING WATER

Throughout the Bible the image of a river is employed as a metaphor for the blessings that come from heaven and give us life. According to the creation narratives, a river flowed out of the Garden of Eden and branched into four tributaries that watered the earth.[6] The book of Psalms begins with a promise that those who delight in the law of the Lord will be "like trees planted by streams of water, which yield their fruit in its season, and their leaves do not wither."[7] After humanity fell into sin, finding the life-giving river from heaven became something of a challenge.

Isaiah referred to this river as thin "streams in the desert," which is how most biblical characters perceived this heavenly river.[8] They were not righteous enough to find this trace of water that could keep their lives from withering. So they continued to thirst—just like we do. Therefore, when Jesus showed up at a well in Samaria one afternoon long ago, promising to provide living water, he was touching the age-old longing of the human soul.

At the end of the biblical story, we find a glorious description of the heavenly river of life. Significantly, it will flow from the throne of God and of the Lamb and only then nurture the tree of life, whose leaves will be used for the healing of the nations.[9] In the end, the river will again be easy to find, and no one who is brought to the shores of heaven will ever thirst again.

All these biblical references to the river consistently make two claims. The first is that we need the water from this river in order to become spiritually alive. The second is that this water can only be given to us by God, because the sacred river flows out of his love. In light of these claims, it makes sense when John states plainly that the river of living water is actually the Holy Spirit. In John 7, three chapters after the account of the woman at the well, Jesus once again speaks about this water:

> "Let anyone who is thirsty come to me, and let the one who believes in me drink. As the scripture has said, 'Out of the believer's heart shall flow rivers of living water.'" Now he said this about the Spirit, which believers in him were to receive; for as yet there was no Spirit, because Jesus was not yet glorified.[10]

The sacred river that has always flowed from the heart of God into our world—but which became impossible to find because we had wandered so far, trying to satisfy our thirst with other things—now finds us in the person of the Holy Spirit, like water flowing down over heaven's banks into our thirsty hearts.

The great church council at Nicea stated that the Holy Spirit *proceeds* from the Father and the Son. This means the Spirit proceeds from the Father and the Son to us in order that we may proceed in the power of the Holy Spirit back home to God. Apart from the Spirit the soul withers, for it is existing apart from living water. Nothing else will suffice, for there is no other way to "taste and see that the LORD is good."[11] *This* Lord is what our parched souls have been craving. So nothing short of the baptismal waters of God the Holy Spirit can begin to quench our thirst.

There is quite a bit of discussion in some quarters of the church about being baptized in the Spirit. Some speak of this phenomenon as a second act of conversion, claiming that we must first accept Jesus, then later accept the Spirit, as if there were two saviors. But this interpretation tears apart the Trinity in a way the Bible never does. Some contend that we are baptized in the Spirit once, when we are converted, while others point to the verses in the book of Acts that refer to repeated fillings of the Spirit. Still others argue that baptism in the Spirit and being filled with the Spirit are not the same thing. I think it is important not to be more clear than Scripture itself is on this point. It's difficult to pin down someone as mysteriously powerful as the Holy Spirit. Clearly there is more of the Spirit's living water to receive than any of us would dare claim to possess.

In addition, some speak of the baptism of the Holy Spirit as though it were synonymous with speaking in unknown tongues and performing signs and wonders, as the apostles did. These things may or may not happen, but they are not promised. What *is* specifically promised is that when the Spirit comes upon us we will receive power. The purpose of this power is to allow us to witness (that is, to watch) what the risen Jesus is now doing in the world and in our lives through the Spirit. It is important not to make the term *baptism* mean more than the Bible itself means when it uses the term. For example, Jesus told his disciples, "John baptized with water, but you will be baptized with the Holy

Spirit."[12] Here Jesus uses the term *baptism* as a metaphor to describe the life-giving ministry of the Spirit in our lives. This is water for which we have been searching, for only this water flows, or proceeds, from God.

Why, then, are so many followers of Jesus still thirsty in spite of all the information they have learned about Jesus and in spite of practicing all their rigorous disciplines? Why do we seem so hesitant to receive this filling of God's Spirit? I would suggest it's not because we are scared of being possessed by God; rather, it is because we are so determined to find the water on our own. Believe me, we can't find it. We can only let it find us by stopping the relentless search long enough to turn our thirst into prayer— and then to wait for the Spirit.

THE NEED FOR AN UPPER ROOM

When the disciples knew they had to wait for the promised gift, they wisely chose to go to an upper room. Luke tells us that the eleven remaining followers, a number of women (including Mary the mother of Jesus), and Jesus' brothers entered the room and devoted themselves to prayer.[13] We don't know if this was the upper room in which they had shared the Last Supper with Jesus. It could have been—but it doesn't really matter. In the New Testament, the *upper room* is a metaphor for a place of spiritual intimacy. It is a room of prayer, which exists in your own heart. It's the kind of thing Jesus was referring to when, in the Sermon on the Mount, he said, "Whenever you pray, go into your room and shut the door and pray to your Father who is in secret."[14] There needs to be an "upper room" in every life, a place in your heart with a door to close, a place where you are not distracted.

It's the place where you find the power of the Holy Spirit—the holy chamber where you are devoted to prayer. John Calvin claimed that the most important reason to pray is so that our hearts might be filled with a zealous and burning desire ever to seek, love, and serve God. We may not think all this prayer is necessary; we may conclude that we simply don't have time for it. After all, we know about Jesus. We are trying our best to be good and faithful disciples. There's a lot of work to do, so why can't we just get at it?

However, when Jesus' followers entered this upper room in Jerusalem, they already knew a lot more about Jesus than we do. They had a clearer sense of calling than we do. They had seen more miracles than we will ever see—and yet they knew they didn't have the power to be of use to God apart from the Holy Spirit. If Jesus' own mother, the blessed virgin Mary, had to devote herself to prayer, chances are good we also need an upper room in our lives.

In reality, we need to spend time in this "upper room" every day. Before we take on the world around us, we need to return to the place where God meets us, opening our lives to the power he alone can give. This is the only way to live freely in this world, because if we do not pay attention to the power within us, we will succumb to the powers around us.

When Luke lists the names of all the disciples devoted to prayer in the upper room, Judas Iscariot's name is missing. Later in the text, we are told about Judas's tragic self-destruction after betraying Jesus.[15] It is striking that, in the process of betraying Jesus, Judas left another upper room in frustration before anyone else did.[16] He was determined, on his own, to do something he thought was better. He left too soon.

If we leave the upper room too soon, unbearably frustrated at having to wait on Jesus and the Holy Spirit, we will always rush ahead to self-destruction. It doesn't really matter how sincere we are or how hard we work; we will end up making deals with others who are in power (which are, in fact, pacts with the devil). For our own "thirty pieces of silver," we will come to the end of life, having betrayed everything we believe in. But if we remain in the room, return to it often, and wait upon the Holy Spirit, we will find the power to make a difference in the world.

It is also in the upper room of prayer that we frequently discover we are waiting for the wrong thing. While the group of believers was gathered for prayer, Peter made a motion to elect a twelfth disciple.[17] They had always been known as "the Twelve," and it bothered Peter that they were now only eleven. So they nominated two candidates, prayed over the selection, and cast lots. The lot fell to Matthias. Great, now they were *the Twelve* again— but immediately after this the Holy Spirit exploded into the place where they were meeting and forced the disciples to face the world around them. After this we rarely hear the disciples described as "the Twelve." Now they were *apostles*, "sent ones," who were soon to go out into the world with their identity now rooted in the Holy Spirit.

In our upper room of prayer, we may think we are waiting on God to give us what we want; it may be healing from a disease or it may be a boyfriend or girlfriend. But when the Spirit comes upon us in our prayers, we discover that we were waiting for the wrong thing. We had settled for small, comfortable dreams, because our prayers had not yet been interrupted by the great dreams of God. Imagine the Spirit coming to us while we waited for a job promotion to say, "Instead of that, how would you like to change the world?"

Pope Gregory I (A.D. 540–604) experienced it. Gregory's dream was to live the quiet, contemplative life of a monk. But as he prayed day after day, he heard God's call to serve the church in a leadership position. So he was disappointed, but not surprised, when the call came to stand for election as pope. He regarded himself as "a contemplative condemned to action." Rome was in shambles when Gregory became pope in A.D. 590. The seat of the empire had moved to Constantinople, so there was to be no help coming from there. The city of Rome had been devastated by famines and invading armies, and the local political authority was weak and corrupt. Seeing what needed to be done, Gregory sold much of the church's vast wealth to care for the poor. He strengthened the church spiritually by renewing its call to be engaged in missions and extended the faith as far as England. He renewed the church's worship life and restored the vision of the clergy to that of "shepherds of souls." Most of the renewal he initiated served to guide the church for the next thousand years. It all began because as a young man he went to his "upper room" each day, asking God to make him a good, anonymous monk.

None of the great leaders of the church ever aspired to greatness. Rather, they aspired to know God and were determined to wait with their thirsty souls upon the Holy Spirit in prayer. History has made these men and women great, but they were all ordinary people, just like you and me. The greatness came not from their gifts and skills, but from the power of the Spirit at work in empty vessels. Emptying is one of the first things that happens in the upper room—but only so that we can be filled.

NO FEAR

Throughout the Gospels, we find Jesus constantly telling people not to be afraid. While being so forgiving of people's many sins and shortcomings, Jesus was always hard on those who were consumed by fear. When people were afraid to give up what they were holding on to so tightly and obey his command to follow him, Jesus turned his back on them and walked away. When the disciples were afraid of the storm at sea and thought they were going to die, Jesus scolded them. When they were terrified, hiding in the upper room after his resurrection, Jesus appeared in their midst and again rebuked them, asking, "Why are you frightened?"[18]

Why is our merciful Savior so consistently hard on those who are afraid? We discover the answer in John's first epistle, which tells us that "perfect love casts out fear."[19] The fear we maintain is the measure of how little of God's love we have received. To be filled with God's Spirit is to be filled with God's love, which makes us unafraid—unafraid even of the cross, where Christ demonstrated his passion, which is another word for love.

Since the ministry of the Spirit is to adopt us into the holy family of the triune God and to give us the Son's own relationship to the Father, we inevitably take on the passions of Jesus Christ. As the apostle Paul said, "It is no longer I who live, but it is Christ who lives in me."[20] So to be filled with the Spirit is to be drawn deeper and deeper into Jesus' passion, even his passion on the cross.

Most of us would love to believe in something enough to be willing to die for it. The reason we don't is not due to a lack of worthwhile causes and missions. Rather, we are too preoccupied with our own thirsty lives. Ironically, the Spirit satisfies our thirst by engrafting us into Christ's dream of sacrificing his life for others. Thus, our fears no longer prevent us from possessing passionate dreams. We have already died to this life—and it's just not possible to scare dead people.

Why were the early church martyrs willing to face lions? Why did the persecuted church outlive the Iron Curtain? Why does the church thrive today in places of greatest resistance? Why didn't any of these believers just crawl into holes and pray for their own salvation? Because they had found in the Holy Spirit transforming power to witness to death-defying hope.

On September 15, 1999, we witnessed yet another senseless crime against children when a deranged man entered Wedgewood Baptist Church in Fort Worth, Texas, and began gunning down the youth groups gathered there for a See-You-at-the-Pole rally. Shortly afterwards, the *New York Times* ran a story about seventeen-year-old Mary Beth Talley. She reported hearing the gunman say, "Your religion is nothing. It's not worth anything. It means nothing." Then he opened fire. As everyone ducked for cover, Mary Beth saw a confused eighteen-year-old girl with Down's syndrome sitting upright because she didn't know what to do. Mary Beth jumped on top of her and said, "You have to be quiet and stay down with me." As she shielded this girl's body with her own, Mary Beth was wounded by gunfire.

There is so much evil in this world, and no shortage of reasons to be afraid. But then we hear such a poignant story: a confused girl with Down's syndrome sitting among a shower of bullets, another girl jumping in the way of the bullets as a testimony to the world that the evil gunman was wrong. Her religion is something. It means everything. It means she is not afraid.

Here we see another illustration of what Jesus meant when he promised that we would receive power through the outpouring of the Spirit. God's power makes us unafraid. When the Spirit exorcises the demonic fear out of our lives, we are free to see that there is nothing, absolutely nothing, that can threaten a Savior who has risen from the dead! Then, and only then, are we able to enjoy the gift of life, for we are no longer crippled by anxiety, by the threat of losing everything.

This may be more power than we really want. I have become convinced that, as much as we fear our hurts and sorrows in life, we fear this power even more. Why? Because if we use God's power we must take responsibility. The last time we tried to do that it didn't work out very well. So we resolved to just take care of our own little garden, to hide in the crowd of the unimpressive who are never to blame. But we cannot be filled with the Spirit and hide our power.

Have you ever noticed that children cannot hide their emotions? No matter whether they are happy or sad, it's written all over their little faces. I think this is true because they are so little; they are smaller than the huge emotions they are trying to contain. It may also account for the inability of little kids to keep a secret. A secret is bigger than they are. One curse of growing up is that we begin to find room in ourselves to hide things behind our mature restraint, adult professionalism, and careful language. Sometimes we hide things so deeply we cannot find them ourselves. But to be filled with God's Holy Spirit is to receive something much bigger than we are, something we cannot contain. Like children, we are free to let this power show through. As dearly loved children of God, we are free to let our gifts be used, to give glory to the God who gave us these wonderful gifts.

No one is as powerful as the person who recognizes who he or she truly is. "All who are led by the Spirit of God," Paul explains, "are children of God . . . and if children, then heirs, heirs of God and joint heirs with Christ."[21] *That's* who you are: the Father's heir, the joint heir of Jesus Christ. That is a description, not of privilege, but of responsibility. In other words, you were not given power in order to try and secure your own life, but to live life as a proclamation to the thirsty souls around you that you know where to find the living water. You have the power, and you certainly have the calling. The question is, will you use it? For that you must return to the Holy Spirit.

STAYING WITH THE SPIRIT

Every time another catalog lands in my mailbox, I am reminded of how deeply rooted the values of consumerism have become in our society. Many marketers today have even reduced our identity to that of *consumers*. Advertisers tell us to be sure to be good consumers, to insist on our rights as consumers, and to work hard at getting a great deal as we consume still more. Some market their products, other market their great service—but they all assume that we are nothing more than people whose primary goal in life is to consume.

More than a few churches have learned these lessons well and now seek to market their religious programs and message as though the Holy Spirit were simply one more thing that could be packaged and sold. I once attended a seminar, along with about a hundred young pastors from around the country, to sit at the feet of a highly respected expert on church growth. Through the entire seminar we lapped up every new creative idea he gave us to bring people into our stores (oops, I mean, churches). At the end of the event, the organizers polled us to determine who we would like to hear from next year. The winner, by a landslide, was Sam Walton, the founder of Wal-Mart!

I agree that congregations should work hard to be evangelistic and seeker-sensitive, but I also believe that the church has been entrusted with the mission of calling people to an encounter with the Sacred. I'm also quite certain we don't do God justice by packaging him and putting him on sale like any other product in a national discount store. When the Spirit fills us, we are not given something else to consume and lose, but we are given God himself.

Those of us who have experienced something of this filling know that only God can satisfy our parched souls, but we are still tempted to revert back to our old habits of consuming. Some of us consume the things we find in catalogs, stores, or showrooms. Others of us are more tempted to consume yet another new relationship, job, or church. Waiting on the Holy Spirit is hard work, and these other things are so available and enticing. *Perhaps something else we find lying around in this world will satisfy our thirst just as well,* we think. But before long, after all this consumption, we feel both bloated and empty at the same time. We have gorged ourselves on other things, but our souls are starving yet again.

It doesn't matter that we know better. We are addicted. We have filled our veins with the narcotics of one more thing for so long that, even though we have known the filling of the Spirit, the inclination to return to consuming other things is always tempting. Like addicts, we have to work our program. We have to return day after day to the "upper room" in prayer, where we wait patiently and remind ourselves that nothing except God's living water will really satisfy us. Only in prayer and worship do we remember that we are powerless over our addictions and that only the Spirit of God can save us.

So I understand why the disciples kept staring up toward heaven after Jesus ascended out of sight. In Jesus they had found a Savior, and they were terrified of facing the world and their sin-addicted lives without him. But that was before they discovered what can happen in an upper room.

CHAPTER
9

THE LONGING TO CONFESS

Have you ever wondered what a pie chart of your time would look like? What percentage of your time is devoted to work? to family commitments? to all the things you have to do: pay the bills, do the laundry, mow the lawn, drive in the car pools? These activities make up the big sections of the pie chart. The smaller slivers of the chart indicate the room that is left for exercise, recreation, volunteering, your friends, and maybe a few spiritual activities.

We live complicated lives that place in front of us a legion of demands every day—and the demands are not just for our time. No, what they are demanding is a larger portion of our hearts. Here is the essence of the integrity problem: We are a people with divided hearts. A large portion of our hearts is dedicated to being successful at work, while another large chunk is dedicated to being successful in relationships. Still another part of the heart would really like to be a successful follower of Jesus, to nurture the life of the Spirit, and to be a student of the Bible. If only we had room in our hearts.

THE DIVIDED HEART PROBLEM

The more of one's heart that goes to one of life's demands, the less that is left for the rest. Now we are confronting what is essentially a math problem. There just isn't much room left over. So we do the best we can in trying to cram it all in. It's as though there is a bad committee meeting going on inside the heart; whenever we get a little free time, everyone in the meeting starts arguing for the surplus: "Me! Me! Pick me!"

When we do give time to one part, we profess to be completely devoted just to it. "Oh, honey, nothing is more important than being with you." "Yes sir, I'll work late tonight to get this project done; it's up to me to make it happen." Then we come to church and confess, "I believe in God the Father, Almighty, Maker of heaven and earth. . . ." The problem is, if we truly believe any one of the preceding statements, we are lying when we say the other two. If no one is more important than your honey, then that includes work and God. If it is up to you to make it happen at work, then you don't really believe in God as the Maker of all things.

Could it be that this is why most of us avoid trying to integrate our lives? We really don't want to face, let alone resolve, the contradictions we are living with. We would rather live with compartments in life, each with its own little lord and its own set of rules. But it is the compartmentalization of life that is largely responsible for our failure with integrity. This is why moral people do immoral things in private. They think that the private compartment should not be judged by the standards of the public ones. Compartmentalizing is also why aggressive people come to church to proclaim belief in God's grace or why good people become vicious in the marketplace: "It's just business. Don't take it personally." We need to be aggressive in the workplace, we believe, but not at home or at church. We think that we should be loving and tender in those places, but we're afraid we won't get far at work by showing any loving tenderness.

Whenever we move from one compartment of life to another, we enter a different world in which we have a different identity. After a while, our souls get worn out, and the walls that divide the compartments begin to break down.

For example, one Sunday morning I was horrified to hear that two of our worshipers got into a screaming match over a parking place in the church lot, then both calmly entered the sanctuary to worship a God who calls us to love and to sacrifice for each other. These two have a problem with integration and, thus, an integrity problem. Even the word *integrity* is derived from *integration*. Only when one's life is integrated does it have integrity.

The Oxford English Dictionary offers two definitions for *integrity*. The first refers to that which is undivided, unbroken, unmixed, and structurally pure. It is in this sense that we speak of a bridge as having "structural integrity." It stands because its supports are solid, pure, sound. The second definition of integrity refers to one who possesses sound moral virtue. We often assume that only the second definition applies to people, but actually both do. We cannot be morally virtuous if we are divided, mixed, or compartmentalized.

So integrity doesn't just mean that we avoid hypocrisy. It means that we have found an integrating virtue to our hearts. In the words of Søren Kierkegaard, "To have a pure heart means to will one thing." In the teaching of the book of Acts, integrity means that we are no longer lying to God, telling him in a church setting that he is Lord, while at the same time holding back a part of our hearts in our daily living.

According to Luke's report, the church in Jerusalem enjoyed a wonderful spirit of giving in its early days. A man named Barnabas sold a field he owned and gave all the proceeds to the church. Others also gave so abundantly that there wasn't a single needy person in the church.[1] Everyone was living completely and totally in the hands of God—well, almost everyone.

A couple named Ananias and Sapphira wanted to be giving people as well. They wanted to live in God's hands, but they were too afraid. So they settled for just appearing to be abandoned to God. Like Barnabas, they sold a field, but they kept back some of the earnings and merely told the church they were giving everything. When their lie was unveiled by Peter, they dropped dead on the spot—perhaps from terror, perhaps from shame. Whatever the case, their failure in integrity cost them their lives.[2] Peter made it clear that it wasn't a sin to keep some of the proceeds from the sale.

After all, the field had been theirs, and they were free to give whatever percentage of the profit they wanted to give. No, the sin was in claiming to be people they were not, in pretending that appearances were enough.

Every time I walk to the pulpit wearing my pulpit robe, the stole around my neck, I am haunted by the words of an elderly woman who once told me, "Son, if you have nothing to say, you ought at least to look nice." We live in a society that dresses up pretty well. We wear power suits instead of blue jeans when we want to feel powerful. But we cannot change the inside by changing the outside. Neither do we become righteous by merely looking righteous. Rather, we become righteous from the inside out, by confessing that we are not right, that our hearts are divided and mixed, and that we are afraid to place all of life in God's hands.

To live with true integrity, with a totally integrated life in which God is God over every part of life and nothing is ever held back, is asking a lot. Frankly, it asks more from us than we can pull off. I understand why Ananias and Sapphira held back some of their money. They had bills to pay, other parts of life to worry about. It's terrifying to give everything to God. What will he do with all of the compartments we have fretted over for so long? Will he ensure that we are a success at work? Will he take care of our loved ones? Maybe we should keep back a portion of our hearts just in case. But we will never have integrity if we withhold even the smallest sliver of our hearts from God. We will spend all of our time on that sliver, trying to make it save us.

The gospel does not require us to muster up the integrity to be right; no, it requires us merely to confess that not a single part of our divided hearts is right. When, however, we tell the truth about this, we discover the deeper truth of the Holy Spirit's power to transform our fears into faith, as we watch him move into every corner of the heart.

We are offered no evidence that Ananias and Sapphira thought they were lying to God. From all appearances they thought they were lying to the compartment of life called *the church*. But God has never accepted our allegiance to the compartmentalization of life. God is Lord over all of our hearts, which means that every lie we tell is told to God. Lying to God is lying to the heart surgeon.

We might as well be dragged out and buried, because we will never be healthy enough to enjoy life. We will waste our lives trying to make the other lords happy; in the end we will still die of a broken heart. But to tell the truth about our need for a Savior at home, at work, and in all our relationships is to discover the integrity of Jesus Christ. Only *in him* do all things truly hold together.

THE JUDGMENTAL PROBLEM

Prior to 1975, many dictionaries did not contain the word *judgmental*. For a number of years now, however, as Dennis Prager noted in *The Wall Street Journal*, "judging evil is widely considered worse than doing evil."[3] It isn't hard to find someone today who says, "You don't need to be judged." "No one has a right to evaluate your lifestyle." "There are no bad ideas." Actually, there are a lot of bad ideas, and to claim that no idea is bad is one of the worst ideas we hear today.

Simply uttering the word *sin* in contemporary culture can conjure up the most primitive emotions within us. Some remember the harsh words of the preacher who melted their self-esteem by repeatedly calling them sinners. It took years of therapy to dig themselves out of that black hole, and they refuse to go back there again. Others question the legitimacy of speaking of sin at all, wondering if it isn't obsolete in modern vocabularies. They prefer that the church speak more tolerantly about "neuroses" or the desperate responses of people who have been hurt.

Now, I'm no fan of sermons that say little more than "bad dog!" but I wonder if Shakespeare might not remind us that we protest our innocence too much. Perhaps we so strenuously refuse to tolerate the "ridiculous" television preacher who just keeps screaming the word *sinner* into our living rooms because we fear he is right.

When John the Baptist was conducting his revival services at the Jordan River, we are told that all Judea came out to hear his message.[4] "Even now the ax is lying at the root of the trees," John the Baptist told his listeners. "Every tree therefore that does not bear good fruit is cut down and thrown into the fire." "So, with many other exhortations, he proclaimed the good news to the

SACRED THIRST
PART TWO — *The Living Water*

people."[5] Good news? How is this good news? Every time I read this text I wonder how my congregation would respond if I used John's words for the Sunday morning call to worship: "You brood of vipers! Who warned you to flee from the wrath to come?"[6] Would they think they were about to be treated to an hour of good news?

They may not call it good news, but in their hearts the congregation would at least know that they are hearing the truth. We have been measured and evaluated from the day we were born and have constantly been told to try harder. When we were children, our parents told us we weren't good enough, and now that we're parents, we're apt to hear the same thing from our kids. Worst of all, we are judged every morning by the person who keeps staring back at us in the mirror. So I'm not surprised that all of Judea came out to hear John berate them. *Sinner? Amen!* we whisper to ourselves. *You preach it, John.* The truth is that we are a lot more like Ananias and Sapphira than we are like Barnabas. We've known it for a long, long time—and all our pretending has only succeeded in wearing down our souls.

After John warned the people of the coming judgment, they didn't argue or protest their innocence. They simply asked, "What then should we do?"[7] John explained that whoever had two coats should share one with someone who had none, that tax collectors should not cheat, that soldiers should not bully people, and that everyone should be content with his or her wages. These prescriptions are striking in their simplicity. John didn't tell these people things they didn't already know. He did not ask them to withdraw into the desert or to do anything heroic. He simply told them to do the right thing. To this list we could add many other things we know to be right: Don't steal time from your spouse or your children. Stop complaining so much. Always be gentle. Give freely to those in need. Honor your commitments. Interestingly, most of the things we know we ought to be doing involve giving. We are expected to give a lot.

When I was in graduate school, I once attended a Christmas party where I noticed that my friend from Korea was using two hands to pass out his presents. I had seen other Asians do the same thing, so that night I asked my friend why he used both hands to pass out his gifts. He said it was more than a matter of being polite. "We always give and receive gifts with two hands because for a moment we share the present, not hiding or withholding anything." Again, that is exactly how God gives to us, with both of his hands—the Spirit and the Son. He holds nothing back. But when we give, we always seem to do so with one hand behind our back. At best.

I will never forget the time I witnessed a wonderful example of two-handed giving. I received a call that Kees Huijssoon, a gentle Dutchman in our congregation, was dying at home. When I arrived, I passed the doctor, who was leaving him for the last time. I did what pastors do in such a situation: I embraced the family, sat down and listened to them, reminded them of the resurrection, prayed, and quoted a few Scripture verses. But the most powerful message in that room came from Mrs. Huijssoon. After forty-nine years of accompanying her husband around the globe, she had spent the last years focusing all of her attention on the overwhelming demands created by one stroke after another. Eventually the strokes robbed her beloved husband of his mind.

Death is never pretty or romantic. It is always messy. It smells bad. It drains all the energy out of those who care for the dying. But as Mr. Huijssoon's life drew to an end, I saw his loving wife caress his brow, moisten his lips with a damp cloth, and whisper comforting words in his ear until he had gone home to be with his heavenly Father. She withheld nothing from him.

The following Friday evening we planned his funeral. One hour later, my wife and I were hosting a group of newly married couples. I could not resist telling them that I had just seen how their marriages would end—if they were blessed. Even now, when I asked Mrs. Huijssoon for permission to tell this story, she granted it right away, then added, "It hasn't always been easy, but it was never a burden. It was just love."

This is what we want. Who doesn't want to spend life giving and receiving this kind of love? The problem is that we have been hurt so many times that we close our hands around our hearts. If you've ever been hurt by someone you once trusted or by someone at work or even by the church, you know how awful it feels. You never want to be hurt like that again. So, instead of really giving yourself to others, you make a fist to shake at any who may try to take something away from you. But when you are clutching at something, you can neither give nor receive love, which always requires two open hands.

Thus, when John tells us simply to do the right thing, we are compelled to say, "I know what I ought to do, but I cannot." The problem isn't *knowing* what we ought to do; the problem isn't even *wanting* to do what we ought to do. The problem is taking the risk in doing it. It's just too frightening. We need help, more help than John the Baptist and his warnings of impending judgment can give us. We need to find someone more powerful than John.

THE DEVIL PROBLEM

Saint Augustine's *Confessions* is perhaps the finest material ever written about the struggles of the human soul. In it, Augustine describes how as a young man he would stare at the pear tree in his neighbor's yard. He wanted his neighbor's pears, even though he had plenty in his own house that were sweeter. After he stole them, he ended up feeding them to the hogs. The allure was not the pears, but the fence that separated them from him. He was fixated on the fruit simply because it was forbidden. In writing about this same dynamic, the apostle Paul once said, "I do not understand my own actions. For I do not do what I want, but I do the very thing I hate.... So then, with my mind I am a slave to the law of God, but with my flesh I am a slave to the law of sin."[8]

I don't preach on sin a great deal. In my experience most of us don't need to be reminded that we are sinners. We are, I think, quite clear about that and about the mess we have made while trying to satisfy our lives with something other than living water. What we are truly confused about is how to find grace.

The reason for our confusion is that we have just too much resolve and too much hope in self-improvement. Assuming we have a higher degree of competency in us than Paul, we decide, "I *will* do the good I want to do; I *will not* do the things I know are wrong." If we are tired of having our lives ruined by the hurt and the resentment we hold against others, we resolve to forgive—but we can't. If we want freedom from our addictions to lust, alcohol, power, or control, we resolve to give up our addictions—but we can't. If we become fed up with having our work consume our lives, we resolve to work harder at not working so hard—but that just doesn't make sense.

The problem with all this resolve, Paul explains, is that evil is right there with us.[9] It isn't just a matter of our good intentions. We are being tempted by an evil force that is determined to make us hurt ourselves. Now, I talk even less about Satan than I do about sin, because I don't want to give time to the devil. But Satan *is* real, and I have plenty of memories of times I jumped fences to get what I didn't really want to prove it.

Some people claim that the devil is just an invention by weak people who need someone to blame for their mistakes. But Satan does not tempt us to self-destruct because we are weak. Generally speaking, he is not worried about weak people. Rather, he tempts us because we are strong and full of resolve to do the right thing. When Paul wrote about this great "civil war" going on within him, he was in the process of writing the most overtly theological book of the Bible. The widespread circulation of the book of Romans poses a profound problem for Satan, so Paul was undoubtedly under siege during the time the Spirit was inspiring him to write this book that shows us how to be made right by God's grace. Do not think for one minute that your good intentions go unnoticed. You have an adversary named the devil, who holds the power of a roaring lion in your life.[10] When it comes to addiction to sin, you will not defeat a roaring lion simply with a little resolve. You're in way over your head on this one.

"Wretched man that I am!" the apostle laments, "Who will rescue me from this body of death?" Without lifting his quill from the paper, Paul immediately answers his own question: "Thanks be to God through Jesus Christ our Lord!"[11] We have a Savior named Jesus, who alone is strong enough to bind Satan! We began the Christian life only by tasting the living water of God brought to us by Jesus Christ—so why do we think we're going to be able to live that life with God by any means other than through that same Savior?

Martin Luther's right-hand man throughout the Reformation was Philip Melanchthon. Philip kept coming to Luther, confessing that he could not rid his life of a particular sin. Luther would give him good counsel, pray with him, and then send him back. Before long they had the same conversation about the same sin. Again Luther ministered to him and sent him back. Philip returned yet another time, still burdened by this sin. Finally in a moment of exasperation, Luther exclaimed, "Melanchthon, the gospel is about Jesus Christ. You don't fight sin by wrestling with the devil, but by turning to the Savior."

THE DESPAIR PROBLEM

If you have ever traveled to Israel, you may have had the opportunity to walk down into Lazarus's tomb.[12] It's a dark, dark place. Actually, even if you've never been to Israel, you have probably been in that tomb at some point in your life. Maybe it was when you lost your job. Or when the doctor tried to explain how the disease was spreading throughout your body. Or when someone you loved broke your heart. But, invariably, the primary reason we find ourselves in Lazarus's tomb is because we have buried ourselves with guilt over the things we have done and the things we have left undone. Yeah, we all know exactly what Lazarus's dark tomb looks like.

The last thing you ever want to do in Lazarus's tomb is get used to being in there. It is, after all, a tomb. Only the dead should be comfortable in there. But getting comfortable is exactly what we try to do when we resign ourselves to an addiction to sin and say, "Well, that's just the way I am. I know I shouldn't have such a temper, but it's just the way I'm wired." No, it's not! You are what God has made you to be, and God did not make you angry. But because we fail to spend enough time by the stream that flows from the heart of God, we despair of ever being able to change. This experience goes to the heart of our great fear that there is no possibility of ever being different. The moment we cave into this despairing thought, the stone rolls across the entrance to our tomb.

Others of us settle into the tomb because we were once hurt so badly that we've lost heart. I have discovered that some of the worst hurts people experience in life come from words that spilled out in anger: "I'm leaving. You just don't deserve my love" (as though anyone ever deserved love). James reminds us, "The tongue is a fire. The tongue is placed among our members as a world of iniquity; it stains the whole body, sets on fire the cycle of nature, and is itself set on fire by hell."[13] I think this may be one reason people like animals so much. They can't talk. But we surely can, and with our nimble tongues we slice away at people's hearts—and when that happens, people have an awfully difficult time forgetting it. This is why pastors typically tell married couples that there are some things they simply must not say. For example, even if a spouse feels it at a particular point in time, he or she must never say, "I just don't love you." These words will never be forgotten, no matter how many times we try to take them back.

When we have been badly hurt, especially by words, the temptation is great to nurture the hurt. Eventually we can become so well acquainted with the hurt that it becomes our best friend. That pretty much guarantees an express lane back into the tomb.

The question is this: Once we find ourselves in the tomb, can we still see the Savior? That's pretty hard. When life goes dark, we can't really see anything, including Jesus. Yet it is precisely the time when we must trust our ears and believe the words proclaimed by the church.

The first thing Jesus does is command us to take away the stone from the tomb. This is the church's task—to prevent despair from becoming a viable option by keeping the door open to the presence of our Savior. We tend to confuse depression with despair. Depression is a medical condition caused by many factors, including chemical imbalances in the brain. It is not a particularly spiritual issue. But despair is a loss of hope—an experience that goes to the heart of the spiritual issue. So in all that it proclaims and does through its mission in the world, the church is constantly fighting hopelessness. We cannot raise the dead, but we can certainly roll away the stone as an affirmation of our insistence on hope.

Standing, therefore, at the open door of your tomb, Jesus calls you by name, "Lazarus, come out!"[14] Come out of your fear and grief and anger. Come forth from the dark place where you've been nurturing all that hurt. You don't have to be a victim. Why are you settling for this?

Now you must make a choice: Will you believe that there is a new life waiting for you out there, or will you settle into this place of death? Maybe you don't think you possess that much faith. Perhaps you can't see your way out of your grief or hurt just yet. Do not wait for faith to come, for there is little power in our faith. Rather, the power is in the Savior, who is calling for you.

It always amazes me, but I've seen all too often that people prefer the misery they know to the mystery they do not. But God will never settle for this response—so he keeps calling us back to worship.

WORSHIPING IN SPIRIT AND TRUTH

When Jesus revealed the depths of the Samaritan woman's thirst by reminding her of her five husbands and her present living arrangements, he got too close to the truth. We can only take so much truth at a time—especially when it is about us.

So the woman attempted to change the subject: "Our ancestors worshiped on this mountain, but you say that the place where people must worship is in Jerusalem."[15] It was a tired old argument that had divided Jews and Samaritans for centuries. Samaritans wanted to worship on Mount Gerizim, near where Jesus and the woman were standing, while Jews claimed that the center of true worship was the temple in Jerusalem.

Like the woman at the well, we can spend our lives disconnected from the real argument we have with life. We can argue about whether or not we really are sinners, or about worship styles, the devil, integrity, and undeserved hurts. But because Jesus loves us so much, he will eventually interrupt these arguments to explain precisely how we can keep our thirsty souls satisfied: only by means of Trinitarian worship. This is what he meant when he told the Samaritan woman, "The hour is coming, and is now here, when the true worshipers will worship the Father in spirit and truth, for the Father seeks such as these to worship him. God is spirit, and those who worship him must worship in spirit and truth."[16] Worship is not the place where we resolve arguments; it's the place where we lay them down and get lost in the wonder of spirit and truth.

What does it mean to worship God "in spirit and truth"? It doesn't mean that we must feel spiritual, or that we must figure out the truth and then cling to it. The *spirit* referred to here is the Holy

Spirit, who proceeds from the Father. When the woman responds to Jesus by asserting that when the Messiah comes, he will explain all things so the truth will finally be known, Jesus tells her, in essence, "Well, that would be me." One of John's favorite designations for Jesus is simply that: *the truth*.[17] Thus, to worship in spirit and truth is to worship God the Father in the power of God the Holy Spirit, who guides us into the truth revealed in God the Son.

Many today, searching for a spirituality outside of orthodoxy, seek to worship just in spirit without the Truth. Theirs is a quest to find some mystery beyond Jesus Christ. However, it is futile to try to feel holy while ignoring our sins, which are in need of atonement. At the same time, attempting to worship just in truth without the Spirit invariably digresses into arguments about who really has the truth. This leaves us embattled and defensive about our right answers, and it ultimately does nothing to relieve our thirst for the living water, which is the Holy Spirit.

When we worship as a people filled with the Holy Spirit who guides us into the truth of Jesus Christ, we are at last carried home to the Father. So the real actor from the beginning to the end of our worship is the triune God. Whether it is an individual who worships alone in the quiet of the morning with an open Bible or the people of God who gather in a splendid sanctuary on Sunday morning, our calling in worship is never more than to open ourselves up to this sacred activity that the triune God undertakes.

Whether or not we recognize this activity is really beside the point. It *is* happening. Our faith does not make the Spirit fill us any more than it makes Jesus the truth. Faith is never more than the means of seeing what God is doing. Through the Spirit God is engrafting us into Jesus' relationship with the Father, renewing our identity as forgiven and beloved sons and daughters.

Thus, the way we experience this union with Christ in worship is simply through confession. Only as we tell the hard truths of our sinful lives do we discover the even greater truth of God's mercy in Jesus Christ. It may be the most important role we have in worship—and clearly the hardest thing for us to do. Our society has taught us quite well how to manage the activities of our lives, but, as King David discovered, the only way to manage sin is to commit more sin.[18] Still, when we confess our failure to be as righteous as John the Baptist tells us we have to be, we are then ready for the Spirit to engraft us into the righteousness of Jesus Christ. It is always as we confess our own inability that we discover the ability of Spirit and Truth.

This is the high drama we are rehearsing every time we gather for worship. By the grace of God we have been rescued from our slavery to sin and set free to live as the Father's own beloved children. In worship, this is what we remember—*who we are* and *whose we are*. Then we also remember that the real argument in life is the one God has with us. Why don't we live as cherished daughters and sons of the heavenly Father? Why do we still look for other things to satisfy our thirsty souls? Why don't we now commit ourselves to the "family business" of bringing others to the well?

We can present no adequate defense to these questions from God. All we can really do is confess once again, acknowledging that we do not act like the beloved children of the Father because, for some reason, it is just too hard to believe that this is who we are.

CHAPTER 10

THE COURAGE TO BELIEVE

We have always had a tendency to confuse *complicated* with *hard*. For example, finding the living water for our thirsty souls is not complicated. We must simply confess that we have wandered far from God in our dogged search to find the water on our own—and that we have hurt others and ourselves along the way. But most of all, we must confess that it was necessary for the Spirit to find us and bring us home to our true family in the fellowship of the Father, Son, and Holy Spirit. None of this is complicated—but it is hard. It requires believing.

THE AGONY OF ANSWERS

When Horace Bushnell began his teaching career at Yale Divinity School, he struggled to increase his faith. He prayed that God would give him more light, thinking that enlightenment was what he needed in order to become a better teacher of ministers. In time, however, Bushnell realized that it made little sense to ask God for more light when he had not yet been faithful to the insights God had already given him. The day this understanding gripped him, he wrote in his diary, "I have moved from the agony of questions I cannot answer to the agony of answers I cannot escape."

Finding truth is no less agonizing than searching for it. But it's a different kind of agony. No longer do we have to wander through the desert in the relentless quest for living water. Now we must settle down next to the small stream we have been given. Finding this disillusioning, at times unbearable, we revert once again to asking questions. It's our best defense against committing ourselves to the very difficult truth we have already received.

Some truths are perfectly clear. Wondering about killing your boss? This isn't exactly a gray area in the Bible. Neither are the many things Jesus taught us about life. For example, he made it clear that love is better than hatred, even when it comes to our enemies.[1] Jesus was never ambiguous about our need for dependency on the love and mercy of his Father. And he kept telling his followers that since life is such a fragile thing, it is best to go ahead and lose it while pursuing things that will make an eternal difference.[2] It's all painfully clear.

What we need are not all of the missing pieces to life's puzzle, but enough courage to live by the clear insights we have. Our lives have been placed into the midst of personal relationships in which we have been called to love and to find joy. We have also been placed in the midst of a dark world that is desperate for any light it can find. There really isn't much question about what we should do in these places. The real question is, will we do it?

Neither is there any question about how to find living water. We don't. It finds us, eventually. But sometimes it waits long enough for us to decide if we really do believe that it finds us in the end. This was what a close friend of mine discovered in his own spiritual journey.

I had the privilege of introducing Kyle to Jesus when Kyle was a college student. After he graduated, life took us in different directions. We corresponded and called each other for a while, but eventually we lost touch. Eighteen years later we discovered we were both living in the Washington, D.C., area, and we had a wonderful reunion.

One day, while having lunch, Kyle told me that his spirituality had been on a tremendous growth curve for many years. He had learned a great deal about the Christian faith, developed an extensive library of religious books, taught Bible studies in his church, and served on various evangelistic and missions projects. He had married a wonderful woman who also followed Jesus, and together they were raising three children in their faith. Kyle had it all, knew it all, and was doing it all. But he confessed to me over lunch, "For the last couple of years I have felt so flat. The Christian life just doesn't work."

Now these kinds of statements have a way of grabbing the attention of pastors, so I asked him to tell me exactly what he meant by *doesn't work*. He quickly reassured me that he wasn't about to leave the church or the faith. But it didn't matter how much he read or understood or achieved, he still couldn't recover his spiritual passion. As tears began to well up in his eyes he leaned across the table and said, "Craig, I just want the fire back. I want to be in love with God again and know that my life is consumed by something of earthshaking importance."

It was not a new conversation for me. More times than I like to recall I have spoken with people who describe their relationship with God as though they were a middle-aged couple who have learned a lot about each other but somehow have lost the passion and head-over-heels feeling of being in love. No one is really satisfied with it, but most of us settle into it.

Kyle was hoping that I would tell him how to restore vibrancy in his faith—but also that I wouldn't give him one more thing to try. In reality, there was nothing left to try, and this fact was the beginning of hope for him. Now it would be possible for all the spiritual disciplines in his life to be used by God, but for far too long Kyle had viewed these disciplines—prayer, Bible study, worship, community, mission—as his means of climbing up the ladder to participate in the bliss of God. However, after years of climbing, it had become painfully clear that he was no closer to heaven than when he began the journey with so much excitement eighteen years earlier. No one ever finds the living water by climbing up.

Human spirituality is, at its best, never more than longing, and after a while, we grow tired of merely longing. What we need is Spirit-uality. Our thirst is for something so sacred that it cannot originate with us or be controlled by us. We find this sacredness not by trying out a new ladder, but by believing that these God-given disciplines can become the channel through which the waters flow down. Only the Spirit can control the flow. Our calling is to believe that if we stay by the dried-out riverbed, the waters will rush down once again.

TRUTH BEHIND THE TRUTHS

Finding the right biblical answers to life's questions is simply one more thing that cannot ultimately satisfy our thirst. In essence, this is what people are often referring to when they say that the Christian life doesn't work. The antidote to our thirsty souls is not a list of propositional truths found in the Bible, but *the* Truth—Jesus Christ—and his living water, the Holy Spirit.

The propositional truths that set our boundaries, describe the nature of God, and define the church's mission are true and binding in their total authority over us. But the purpose of everything the Bible tells us is to reveal the grace of God in Jesus Christ, our true hope. So when we confess that the Bible is the infallible Word of God, we are referring not only to its teachings about how we should live, but even more to its capacity for bringing us home to the Father. All Scripture is inspired by the Holy Spirit, but the ministry of the Spirit is not just to write a sacred book. Rather, the Spirit uses the Bible to engraft us into the beloved Son's relationship with the Father.

So we must always read the Bible at two levels. We read it as a guide for how we should live, obeying it as an act of love for God, and confessing and repenting when we fail to obey. But we must also read the Bible as God's own sacred drama with respect to our thirsty lives. When we read of Adam and Eve reaching for the forbidden fruit, we must see ourselves right there with them, reaching for more than we were ever created to have and losing paradise along the way. It is *we* who are standing on the shores of the parted Red Sea, frightened of the slavery that lies behind but even more terrified of moving into God's strange future. *We* are the ones wandering aimlessly through the wilderness, flirting with other gods, complaining about the hardships.

When we read the New Testament, we join Mary in being frightened and perplexed by this miracle the Holy Spirit has conceived in our lives. Our names might just as well be listed along with the bumbling disciples who keep trying to talk Jesus out of going to the cross. The reason we are so hard on Judas is because there is a traitor chromosome in all of us, which we fear and despise. We are all on the road to Emmaus, so lost in our despair that we cannot recognize the risen Jesus who accompanies us on the journey.

The Bible is a historical record not just of what God has done but of what he is doing. The Jesus we read about in the Bible is the same Jesus who rose from the dead, is now seated at the right hand of his Father, and is still at work in the world through the Holy Spirit. As we come to recognize his presence with us through the Spirit, we can then see that nearly anything can happen in our lives. We can even be overwhelmed with spiritual passion in ordinary places such as at our jobs, as Jesus' disciples discovered.

JESUS IS IN YOUR BOAT

One morning, after Simon Peter and several coworkers had been up all night fishing, they docked their boat without a single fish on board.[3] Remember, these guys weren't fishing for sport. This was the one thing they were supposed to be good at. It was what they did for a living. So when the disciples had nothing to show for their all-night fishing trip, they were feeling a great sense of failure. Just about the time they had their nets cleaned, Jesus showed up with a crowd of people tagging along. He asked Peter if he could use the boat for a pulpit from which to speak to the crowds. Peter agreed, perhaps thinking they might as well use the boat for some productive purpose.

Jesus gave his sermon, looked at Peter, and said, "Now, let's go fishing." "Jesus, you are an incredible teacher," Peter responded, "but I know about fishing, and I'm telling you that we've been at it all night. If we go back out on that lake, we won't catch a thing."

We all have some area of life where we are the experts. It might be raising children or making money—or whatever we do that makes us feel like a success during the week. It is often in these situations that we encounter the most difficult challenge in following Jesus. We may enjoy his message of Good News on Sunday, but the next morning we're inclined to tell him that we know a good deal more about our jobs than he does. But to separate Jesus' teaching from the area in which you happen to be the expert has the effect of turning weekly worship into spiritual entertainment, a delightful distraction from doing what it takes to make a living—as if humans could ever *make* a living.

You can maintain for a while this illusion of being an expert, but what will you do when you come to the harsh realization that, even after all your hard work, you still have empty nets? You have been fishing for success in your job or within your family relationships for a long time. You've tried as hard as you can, but eventually you discover that you haven't caught a thing. You don't feel like a success at work or at home. And you certainly don't feel like a success in your spiritual life because it is the one place where you feel least like an expert. This, thankfully, is the moment when Jesus always appears to encourage you to try it one more time.

After complaining a bit, Peter eventually said, "Nevertheless, if you say so, Jesus, I'll let down the nets again." The word *nevertheless* is such a wonderful word. It's another term for *faith*, which always makes room for our doubts but in the end chooses to do what Jesus asks. "Jesus, I have done all I can do, and I don't see how this could possibly work. There is no hope out there for me; *nevertheless*, if you say so, I will try again." It is all that Jesus asks, and it is all that he requires: "When they had done this, they caught so many fish that their nets were beginning to break. So they signaled their partners in the other boat to come and help them. And they came and filled both boats, so that they began to sink."[4] Incredible.

It would be easy to pass this off as just another fish story that got out of hand, but a net-breaking catch of fish is not the real miracle Luke wants to tell us about. Many biblical commentators knock themselves out trying to explain how it was possible for a school of fish to swim into the nets, and how these ancient boats weren't designed for such massive loads, and . . . and . . . and it all misses the point. The truly amazing part of this story is the claim that there is a Savior in your boat. The focus of this story, the focus of *your* life's story, all turns on that realization. If you believe that the Savior is in your boat, then anything is possible.

Jesus is with you through the storms of life when your little boat is about to sink, and he is with you through the long dull days when your boat drifts aimlessly out to sea. Jesus is with you when you are lost and don't know how to get back to shore, and he is with you when you have fished all night and caught nothing. If you can see that this Savior will not be content to stay along the shores of life to host a nice worship service for you, but insists on going with you back to work—if you can only believe that—then you have every reason to expect some miracles.

Peter was overwhelmed by this discovery. Recognizing that this was *God in the flesh* who was with him, he confessed that he was not worthy to be in the presence of the Holy One: "Go away from me, Lord, for I am a sinful man."[5] No longer did Peter discuss his own expertise or what he had to offer Jesus. He was able to get the right assessment of himself as a sinful man only when he saw who it was that was accompanying him at work. Now he became humbled, even frightened, as his thirst to encounter holiness was quenched.

To have a Savior with you at work, at home, and in the most important places of your life is undeniably a source of great hope—but it can be terrifying to have that much hope. If God has chosen to be in your boat (and this reality is exactly what the story of Jesus proclaims), then your life will never again be the same.

So it was for Peter. His life changed forever, for at that very moment he received his true vocation. "Do not be afraid," Jesus reassured Peter. "From now on you will be catching people."[6] What exactly does it mean to *catch people?* The Greek word used here *(zogreo)* means "to capture alive, to rescue." Those who catch people do not let them fall. Every time the Bible depicts a conversion experience, it begins with a discovery of God and ends with a discovery of mission. The purpose of a worshipful encounter with the Holy Spirit is not just to be reassured that God is with us but also to be commissioned with a sacred calling. After you learn that the Savior is on board with you, you can no longer see yourself as just a fisherman, teacher, banker, homemaker, administrator, or whatever it is you spend your days doing. One of these may be your job, but your vocation is to catch people so they do not fall.

All around us people are falling into despair and cynicism, and in the process they're becoming so much less than they could be. The only thing that will help them is to see that Jesus, the Savior, is with them. But before you can show them that Jesus is with them, you first have to believe that he is with *you*. And the only way you will possess this belief is through continuing to pray, study the Bible, and worship—especially when you are catching nothing. Then the sacred waters can flow, and some wonderful miracles will begin to unfold.

THE HEART OF THE STRUGGLE

Much has been written about our struggle to believe. For many the struggle is presented as an *intellectual* problem that causes us to doubt. For this reason some theologians have tried to make the case for the reasonableness and rationality of our faith. Others claim that this intellectual approach misses the point, for the real struggle, they say, is an *emotional* problem with fear. Those who are convinced that fear is the roadblock to faith do all they can to present Jesus as the Good Shepherd who leads us through the dark valleys. "See," they declare, "there's nothing to fear." Or they speak about hell and judgment in even more fearful terms than they speak about our walk of discipleship with God. But that only reduces faith to a less terrifying option than hell.

When Augustine wrote about his own struggle to believe, he presented yet a third obstacle to faith, which gets closer to the heart of the problem. The struggle, Augustine claimed, is not ultimately with either our intellectual doubts or our emotional fears, but with our *wills*. Clearly we find this to be the core issue for the people Jesus encountered as he walked this earth. He didn't typically begin by telling people, "Don't doubt" or "Don't be afraid." Those messages came later, along the way. Jesus began with the words, "Follow me," which requires an act of the will.

Augustine also maintained that our greatest enemy in this struggle with our wills is *habit*. He writes, "My will was perverse, and lust had grown from it, and when I gave into lust, habit was born, and when I did not resist the habit, it became a necessity."[7] Sin is anything that keeps us separated from God, and it is very addictive. What begins as a single act often becomes a habit, and then a necessity. Because this attachment prevents us from following Jesus, it is the first thing he asks us to give up in order to follow him. It isn't just that Jesus wants us to sacrifice, but, more to the point, that he wants us to believe that our salvation comes exclusively from him and not the other things that, by means of habit, we have made necessary in our lives.

One of our favorite responses to Jesus is to tell him that we are going to believe. We will make the required changes and start to follow him—tomorrow. Augustine knew this approach well: "I prayed to you for chastity and said, 'Give me chastity and restraint, but not yet,' for I was afraid that you would answer my prayer at once and cure me too soon of the disease of lust, which I wanted satisfied and not quelled."[8] It is like telling ourselves that we are going to begin a diet tomorrow. We know what we have to do, so it's not that we aren't clear about the truth of the matter. And we know it is only for our salvation that Jesus invites us to believe in his grace. But we keep postponing the moment of receiving his grace, because the will to believe that only Jesus can bring us the living water of the Holy Spirit is weighed down by our habitual belief that something else can satisfy our parched souls.

Some theologians call this "the hesitation before birth." We know that Jesus is "the way, and the truth, and the life."[9] But we hesitate before fully believing it—maybe we keep hesitating for our entire lives. The other attachments remain a necessity in our lives, and, as a result, so does the thirst.

Thus Augustine challenges us, "Why do you try to stand on your own strength and fail? Cast yourself upon God and have no fear."[10] The fear, as well as the doubts, evaporate only after we choose to cast ourselves on the strength of God. We will never come up with enough belief to talk ourselves out of the habit of unbelief. Salvation comes, then, not through resolve, but through surrender.

Early in my ministry at National Presbyterian I became absolutely overwhelmed with both doubt and fear. I had serious doubts that I would succeed; I had fears that those who were sure I would fail were correct. The doubt and fear had become habit-forming, leading me to think that these emotions were necessary for my pastorate here. Worse, I wondered if all of us had misread God's calling. Perhaps I wasn't even supposed to be here. It didn't help a bit to try to overcome these doubts and fears with firm resolve, hard work, efforts to prove myself, attempts to make myself more lovable to the congregation or to make them more lovable to me. Through it all my own relationship to God was in great turmoil. *Did I even know him? How could I have misread something as important as his sovereign will?*

I expressed these struggles and questions once to an older, retired minister who has been a pastor to me for a long time. Maybe I was looking for some piece of advice that would fix everything; maybe deep down I was hoping he would tell me nothing of the sort—because I knew there was nothing left to try. After listening to me for quite a while, he sat back, smiled knowingly, and said two simple words: "Give up." Shocking words, but he went on to explain that in every church he had served, the turning point in his relationship with the congregation came the day he simply surrendered. He was compelled to surrender to the church just as it was—and thus give up his habit of dreaming that it would be something else. Harder yet, he had to surrender to the man he was and give up the habit of trying to be what the congregation wanted.

Surrender. It isn't terribly complicated, but it is so very hard because it requires that we believe the Holy Spirit will do what we cannot do.

In the subsequent years of my pastorate at this church, all kinds of changes have taken place, both in the congregation and in me. But none of that would or could have happened until I stopped trying to make it happen. I couldn't give up the habit of resolve any more than the habits of fear and doubt—until I first chose to believe the gospel I preach every Sunday.

BELIEVING IS SEEING

Wouldn't you love to see the risen Jesus clearly enough that believing would come quickly and easily? If only we could physically see Jesus with our own eyes, we would never have any doubts. We would believe so easily.

All of the Easter Scripture passages make it clear that the first disciples believed only because of what they saw. John believed when he saw those folded graveclothes in an empty tomb, while Mary Magdalene believed when she saw the risen Jesus face-to-face. The rest of the disciples believed when they saw Jesus in the house in which they were hiding.[11] All of them, that is, except Thomas, who wasn't home when Jesus appeared; he was out running some stupid errand and missed the excitement. All Thomas saw was a lot of breathless exhilaration from the others, who insisted they had just seen Jesus, who was risen from the dead.

I hate not being in the room when miracles occur. I hate having to trust secondhand reports. Like Thomas, I want to see for myself.

In April of 1998, a series of tornadoes ripped through the southeastern part of the United States, spreading destruction and death all across the countryside. The day after one of the tornadoes hit, the National Public Radio program *All Things Considered* aired a story about a congregation called the Church of the Open Door, whose building was destroyed during the storm. Terrified children had been at choir rehearsal at the time. When the pastor saw the tornado coming, he quickly gathered all the children into the church's main hallway. There they had huddled together while the winds tore their church apart. In an effort to calm the children's fear, the pastor had led them in singing "Jesus Loves the Little Children." Although some of the children were hurt, miraculously no one was killed.

The most penetrating part of the broadcast was the report of a little girl who said, "While we were singing, I saw angels holding up the hallway. But the winds were so strong that the angels shouted out 'We need help!' and some more angels came and helped them." What a story! This little girl will never forget what she saw. She will always believe that there are angels watching over all the little children. And if the angels are having trouble, they just call for reinforcements, and more angels come running, because we are precious in the eyes of Jesus.

It was an amazing report. But I missed it. I wasn't in the room when the angels showed up to take care of the children. All I have is a secondhand report from a child. I would give anything to have seen what she saw. I would even be willing to let a tornado tear our own church apart if, in the process, all of us got to see a bevy of angels protecting us. The trustees may have a different opinion, but I would be willing. To see angels? You bet I would. Angels are very popular right now, but I must admit I've never seen one— or at least not that I'm aware of. All I have are a lot of secondhand reports—sort of like the report of angels being present at the empty tomb.

So I understand how Thomas felt. It didn't matter what the others had seen. Until I see Jesus myself, he had said, and put my finger in the nail holes, I do not believe.[12]

"I do not believe." As a pastor, I hear these words a lot. "I do not believe I can ever be in love again, not after what I went through in the last relationship." "I do not believe I will ever be healthy, not after what the doctor told me." "I do not believe I will ever get out of this detestable job, not with all the bills I have to pay and all my family responsibilities." "I do not believe that peace will ever come to the Middle East." All of the doubt and fear is rooted, whether we want to admit it or not, in our inability to believe in Jesus' resurrection from the dead. If we were convinced that the grave was not able to hold Jesus, we would not be surprised to discover that he is still at work in our lives and in the world.

The resurrection of Jesus' corpse back to life means that God has entered this life and has provided real hope for our real problems. Jesus' bodily resurrection proclaims that God makes a response to bodies that do not work and are riddled with disease, to abused bodies and lonely bodies, and to people who feel like they are a nobody. It is the basis for everything we have to say about the sacredness of human life, about our mission and our concern for others, and about joining in the battle to defeat the powers of injustice. Why? Because in the resurrection of Jesus, God has proclaimed that this world matters to him. God is with little children huddled together through the storms of life, and he is with the frightened people of Africa, the Middle East, and North Korea. God is with every one of his children—red and yellow, black and white, they are *all* precious in his sight. If Jesus Christ can defeat death, nothing can stop his great resolve to save our lives. The world is filled with possibility!

This is exactly what we want to believe. And it is why, like Thomas, we desperately need to see this risen Jesus for ourselves. We are told that Thomas was also called "Didymus" (Greek, *Didymos*), which means, "the Twin."[13] We don't know a thing about his twin. It could be anyone—maybe even you. All you have are secondhand reports. It isn't that you don't want to believe them, but you find belief so difficult that you could be Thomas's twin.

Well, Thomas got his wish. A week after Jesus rose from the dead, he appeared to Thomas and said, "Put your finger here and see my hands. Reach out your hand and put it in my side." Confronted with the wounded, risen Christ, Thomas could only exclaim, "My Lord and my God!" But Jesus wasn't finished yet, and he said to Thomas, "Have you believed because you have seen me? Blessed are those who have not seen and yet have come to believe."[14]

Now why would this be? If the resurrection of Jesus is so important, why is it more blessed to believe *without* seeing? Because as long as we cannot see with our eyes, the possibility for faith exists, which is precisely what a loving relationship requires. There were many who saw Jesus with their own eyes, even after the resurrection, but who still never believed that he was their Savior. This deeper relationship with him comes only by choosing to believe. If your spouse or your closest friends had to prove their undying love for you, it wouldn't be much of a relationship, would it? Loving relationships, such as the one God insists on having with us, can only survive by means of a faith that is strong enough to wrestle through the doubts and fears until we find the courage to believe.

If you do not have that much faith, or if your faith is rocked in times of crisis, then you need to follow Augustine's example and ask God for it—for even faith, our courageous choice to believe, is really a grace that flows from heaven as well.

CHOOSING TO BELIEVE BEFORE THE CRISIS

Although the ability to believe is a gift from God, there are things we can do to help us receive this precious gift. All of the spiritual disciplines of worship, Bible study, service, and praying without ceasing throughout the day are ways of positioning ourselves near the river of living water. However, they are *not* the water, and we will remain thirsty if we become more preoccupied with our prayers than with the One to whom we are praying. But they do place us next to the thin stream that flows by our corner of life's desert. This is what the psalmist means when he states that the righteous are like trees planted by streams of water.[15] There we drink in and absorb the grace of the Spirit, who alone can keep us spiritually alive. The more time we spend by the stream, the more rooted we will become in our belief.

Those roots to faith are pretty important, because, quite frankly, sometimes we receive more grace than we want. It doesn't happen often, but when the storms come, the stream can suddenly turn into a raging river, washing away everything that is not firmly planted. We never want to get too sentimental about grace. While most days it is God's gentle refreshment to our souls, sometimes the river comes as a terrifying reminder that our lives are out of control.

On stormy days, we may wonder if it was such a good idea to live so close to the stream. We may even wish that God would just leave us alone. But if the storm sweeps away everything that is not spiritually rooted, then even that is a grace. The point of God's grace is not to be nice to us but to do for us what we cannot do for ourselves. It carries us home to God, sometimes on a gentle stream, sometimes on a raging torrent, but always back to God.

A few years ago two friends buried their seven-year-old daughter, who was killed in a car accident that also put their two sons in critical condition in the intensive care unit. At the little girl's funeral the father stood up to speak about the faithfulness of a God he did not understand. He didn't testify to God's faithfulness just because he knew it was the right thing to do—you see, the right words never get anyone through a crisis. Rather, this couple survived the torrent only because long before this crisis they had chosen to believe these words they were now articulating. They had spent most of their lives next to the river that flows from heaven. Now, in the midst of distress, their lives were so firmly rooted in the Spirit that they couldn't stop believing—even if they had wanted to.

Fred Craddock has asserted that sometimes we believe *because* of what God does, while other times we believe *in spite of* what he does: "Faith is in part a mystery because faith is trust, and who can explain the origins, the vitality, the dynamic, the tenacity of trust one person has in another? Trust has its reasons, to be sure, but it also bears its wounds."[16]

As in any relationship, we choose to keep trusting only because of another mystery: We love the person we are trusting.

PART
3

SATISFYING THE THIRST

CHAPTER

11

FINDING A
HOLY PEOPLE

As we come to believe that the Holy Spirit alone can fill our thirsty souls, we are set free from seeking this living water at other wells. The church is one of these "other wells." It cannot satisfy our thirst, for it is never more than a community of thirsty people. But when we return to this community, no longer expecting it to be more than it is, we are able to receive the gifts it has for us. Foremost among the gifts of spiritual community is the help it gives us in shaping our identity closer and closer to the image of Jesus Christ.

If truth be told, the church usually fulfills this holy ministry in spite of itself.

THE DILEMMA OF CONSTRUCTING OURSELVES

Not long ago I received a tattered old photo album from my aunts. Without a single word, the pictures tell the story of six generations of my ancestors who lived on the same family tobacco farm in North Carolina. Every picture in the album was taken on that farm except one: a photo of my grandfather, Clarence Solomon

Barnes, as a young man. It was taken in Miami. In the photo, he is sitting on a giant crescent moon, looking more than a little lost.

In the midst of all the rural, pastoral scenes in this album, this one picture really stands out. As a child I sat through a lot of stories about the family farm but never heard anything about Granddad hanging the moon in Miami. So I asked my aunts what it was all about.

Early in his life, my grandfather became fed up with life on the farm. So when he was old enough to be on his own, he jumped on a bus and joined one of the big bands touring the South. It was his lifelong dream, but it didn't last long. When he discovered that life in the band was typically accompanied by alcoholism, gambling, and loose women, he quickly became disenchanted. He recognized that this was not who he was. So the "prodigal son" returned to a farm he would never leave again.

In his childhood my grandfather had received a clear view of his true self. Before he ever left the farm, his identity had already been shaped by his parents and the members of his extended family, who all worked the nearby farms; by his teachers and the preacher of the Rocky Mount Baptist Church; and by his lifelong girlfriend—who said she would become his wife only after he had gotten this ridiculous idea out of his head. The community told him who he was, and the only time he wandered away, trying to be someone else, was the time he discovered that he was, after all, a farmer.

It's not a unique story, though it is becoming rarer every day. In contemporary society, we no longer look to our communities and our families for our identity. Instead, most of the time we simply look inside ourselves as individuals and ask ourselves, who do we want to be? Not just what do we want to *do*, but who do we want to *be?*

After seminary my first assignment in ministry was to serve as a college pastor. In this capacity I attended more graduation ceremonies than anyone should ever have to attend. To make matters worse, most commencement speakers said essentially the same thing: "The world stands before you, aflame with opportunity. Dream your own dreams; do your own thing. Work hard, and you can be whatever you want to be."

The effect of all this advice is that we no longer think of ourselves as having a true self to which we can either be faithful or rebel against for a while. Now we think of the self as something that each of us must construct. Pick a school, a spouse, a town, your friends. Pick a job. Pick another job. Soon you can even pick what color hair and eyes you want in your children. It's all up to you to engineer your life, without any influence from the generations that preceded you or the community that surrounds you. "Be whatever you want to be."

We have tried for some time now to live these untethered, weightless lives, floating from one identity to another, unencumbered by any memory of "the father's house." But how have we fared in our attempts to construct our own lives? Half of our marriages are not working out. We are seriously in debt, but we just keep consuming because we desire more things. We've abandoned the antiquated concept of *neighbor* in order to look for friends on the Internet—and still we remain lonely. Many of us hate the jobs we've picked, not because they are really so bad, but because we expected them to be much more than a job. After my grandfather died, I asked my grandmother if he was fulfilled in his work. She thought it was the oddest question. But we know what it means, and we seek fulfillment in work like it was the Holy Grail.

It is hard work constructing one's own life. After trying it for a few decades, we have, in all honesty, gotten a little tired of ourselves and have developed grave doubts that we are ever going to find that elusive fulfillment. Why? Perhaps it is because we have taken our yearnings far too seriously.

In a refreshingly different commencement address, Pulitzer Prize-winning journalist Charles Krauthammer advised the graduates of McGill University in Montreal, "You have been rightly taught Socrates' dictum that the unexamined life is not worth living. I would add: the too-examined life is not worth living either. Perhaps the previous ages suffered from a lack of self-examination. The Age of Oprah does not."[1] If you have ever spent an afternoon watching daytime talk shows, you know what Krauthammer is talking about. It no longer matters how you construct your life, or how many people you hurt along the way, or what absurdly silly things you are doing with life—as long as you are sincere, we are all supposed to clap for you. But even Caligula got bored after a while.[2]

It really doesn't matter why it happens—whether we've simply become bored with the identity we created for ourselves or, like the prodigal son, we've spent everything chasing our dream— eventually a day comes when we turn around and head for home. Some of us yearn to go home because it was a delightful place, and it is so easy to remember who we are when we're there. Others of us recognize that we will never be able to return to the place we were raised, but we still yearn to find a place that looks like the home we've always kept in our hearts. Home isn't necessarily the place we *want* to go; it's the place we *have* to go because, well, it's home.

This truth is pretty much what my grandfather discovered in Miami. Having chased his dream all the way down to the bottom, he discovered that it wasn't much. So he went home. He didn't go home because the farm suddenly became an irresistibly delightful place, but because he knew it was where he belonged. It was the only place where he could really be himself.

The Samaritan woman experienced the same tug. After she encountered Jesus at the well, she ran back to town to tell the people that she may have found the Messiah.[3] Remember, now, that it's a pretty good probability that this community had been extremely hard on her because she was such a failure at marriage and was, even now, living with a man. In all likelihood, men in the community had used her and women had judged her—and she was undoubtedly lonelier in her community than any of us have ever felt in our church community. She had every reason to want to stay with Jesus at the well and to forget about the grief she had been receiving from others in the town. But as soon as she caught just a glimpse of who Jesus really was, she was in such a hurry to shout this good news to her community that she left her jar at the well and raced home to start spreading the hope around. Why? Because it was home.

THE STORY BEFORE YOUR STORY

It is home. This explains why people come to church in the first place, as well as why they keep coming back, even after wandering away for a long time. It is their spiritual home, and there is simply no way to be who they are in the family of Christ apart from this community that tells their story.

When I take a long, hard look at all the somber faces of the dirt farmers in my family photo album, I see myself there. It doesn't really matter that these people are not the most delightful, beautiful, or promising ancestors a person could have. They're family. *My* family. And I simply can't understand who I really am apart from them. Their blood flows through my veins; their genes shaped my body. Their faithfulness, and even their sins, says the Bible, were passed down to me from four generations back.[4] We may despise saying this in our individuality-crazed time in history, but the story of my life began long before I showed up on the scene.

In a frantic effort to buttress our families, many of which appear to be coming apart at the seams, there is a lot of interest in reclaiming the biblical understanding of family. But we must remember that the biblical ideal of a family does not look at all like the Ozzie and Harriet images we had in the 1950s. For one thing, the current image of a nuclear family—a father, a mother, and 2.5 children—is completely foreign to ancient societies, whose homes included extended family members.[5] More important, Jesus revolutionizes the whole idea of "family," claiming that our primary allegiance is to the family of faith. In fact, when Jesus' mother and brothers came to see him, probably in order to rescue him from his busy schedule, he declared that "whoever does the will of my Father in heaven is my brother and sister and mother."[6]

How many times haven't you heard a preacher tell us that our first priority in life is to God, the second to our families, and the third to our work? But a close reading of the Bible reveals a different order. Yes, our first priority is God the Father, but there really are no other priorities. As we call ourselves sons and daughters of this heavenly Father, we find that he has given us brothers and sisters in the faith who share our work in the "family business." But none of this is ever more than a way of calling God our Father. So the challenge for those who want to hang on to their biological families is to bring these family members with us into the new family of faith.

It is precisely because *family* forms and shapes the story of our lives that we are invited into the holy family of Father, Son, and Holy Spirit. As the Spirit engrafts us into the Son's own relationship with his Father, we discover that we are being molded into a new identity—into the very image of Jesus Christ himself. But this shaping never happens outside of the body of Christ, which is the church.

Thus, to understand who we are becoming in Christ, we must take a long, hard look at the biblical pictures of the Father, Son, and Spirit. We must also look at the pictures we are given of all those who were adopted into this holy fellowship centuries before we were. And we have to look at those with whom we share a pew each Sunday morning, looking hard enough to see past the things that distinguish us to discover those traces of family ties. Our brothers and sisters are not there because they deserve to be—but then again, neither are we. Rather, all of us have been adopted into the family by the blood of Jesus Christ.[7] So every time the family gathers around the Lord's Table, we remember *who we are*. As we eat the bread and drink from the cup, Jesus' blood flows through our veins, his righteousness shapes and molds our lives, and his mercy is visited upon us from one generation to the next.

This story, which is now forming your life, began before you showed up, and all of the really important parts of the story have either already occurred or will occur long after you are gone. Creation, the Fall, the raising up of a covenant people to be God's precious possession, the birth, death, and resurrection of the Savior—all of these happened long ago. Yet they are your solid basis for hope in the fleeting chapter called *your life*. According to the book of Revelation, the end of the story has also been written, and it ends wonderfully. There is nothing we can do to make the ending any better than God has already determined it will be. So what we have in the meantime is this "in-between" time and this spiritual community called the church, which can help us remember how to live as though this really *is* our family story. Which it is.

COMMUNITY AS REALITY

In the end it doesn't really matter how flawed the church family is. Even a dysfunctional family can mold our lives in wonderful ways—as long as it is regularly interrupted by the Savior. This insight was wonderfully expressed by the German pastor Dietrich Bonhoeffer. He had watched the church in Germany capitulate to Hitler and the Nazi regime—so he certainly knew something about a flawed family of faith. Bonhoeffer resisted this regression by participating in the underground Confessing Church, but he never thought of this move as a flight into a "pure church." He cautioned his readers to remember that our spiritual family, our *community*, as he called it, is not a human ideal but a divine reality. Nothing, he cautioned, is more dangerous to authentic community than our dreams, because we will always love our dreams more than the community we have been given by God.[8]

To say this does not mean, of course, that our particular community doesn't need to be improved on or disciplined at times, but it does mean that any real change will come only through Christ, who promised to be present wherever two or three are gathered in his name. When Saint Augustine was writing against the Donatists, who were arguing that those who belonged to the church must be perfect or they should be expelled, he reminded them that the body of Christ is holy only because Jesus, its Head, is holy, never because the members of the body take pride in their own righteousness.

Because Jesus Christ is the head of every community that gathers in his name, the dynamic of the family is not abandoned to the dysfunctions of the brothers and sisters but is determined by the Head of the family. As we sit in church and fix our eyes on the cross, we remember that this is who we are. What matters is not who we dream of being, or who we may appear to have become, but who God created us to be *in Christ*. There is no way to discover this identity apart from the work of the Holy Spirit, who always brings us into the family. There is no "only child" in the holy family, not even Christ. We are the adopted "joint heirs" of this only begotten Son, along with all the others the Spirit has gathered into the family.[9]

As we come to the point where we can accept our community as it comes to us in the church, such as it is, we are accepting God's gift to us. Moreover, we also discover that we are accepting ourselves. All of this means that we don't have a clue about who we are in Christ apart from the community.

So, while the church can never satisfy our thirst to encounter God, it can nurture the thirst, point us to the thin stream that flows from heaven, and even remind us of who we are in Christ. As we cling to each other, we remember that we are never going to find in each other what God alone can give us—and this realization frees us to finally enjoy the community for what it is rather than to despair over what it is not.

The apostle Paul often compared the Christian life to running a race. Once he wrote, "Run in such a way that you may win. . . ."[10] This is pretty much the point of entering the race, isn't it? When you're halfway through the race, it isn't a good time to check your pulse, to ask others how you look, or to wonder why in the world you entered this race. You simply want to remain focused on the finish line. It is the only way you can possibly win.

I am surely not an apostle, but I would dare to add that, not only is the Christian life a race, it's a three-legged race. Remember those crazy events? Two kids tie one of their legs together, put an arm around each other's shoulders, then hobble and trip their way toward the finish line, where they collapse in a fit of laughter. I doubt we'll ever see this sport in the Olympics. It tends to show up more frequently at church picnics. (I have no proof of this, but I think three-legged races were probably invented by the church. It is one of our better metaphors.)

You see, we are tied to each other. Consequently, we cannot run as fast as we could if we were on our own. But at least we always have someone's arm around our shoulder. All of Paul's inspired advice still applies. We run to win the race. We surely don't wonder about how we look. We must stay focused on the goal. But at the end we aren't thinking about the glory—because we're laughing way too hard!

DEALING WITH "THE RABBLE"

When the Hebrews left Egypt, they brought with them some people who had no vision for the Promised Land. These folks were called "the rabble."[11] They constantly complained about the hardships of the journey, about Moses, even about God. This rabble didn't consist of a great number of people, but they still created enormous problems. No matter how many miracles God performed, the rabble always seemed to be able to convince the rest of the people to focus more on their fears than on God's faithfulness. In order to accomplish this, they appealed to the people's longing for certainty, permanence, and abundance—all things we must leave behind when we set out on our journey with God.

There has a been a rabble in every church I have served. They don't have to be large in number in order to make their voices known. It doesn't matter how much you do for them, how diligently you try to accommodate or appease them, they simply will not be satisfied, because the whole point of being "the rabble" is to resist the journey the community has undertaken. It is easy to get hurt when you confront a member of the rabble, even to the point of concluding that you must be in the wrong church. "How can this be the body of Christ?" we ask. "Don't these people care about anything other than standing in the way of change?" But even the question itself exaggerates the importance of the rabble—which is exactly what they are hoping you will do.

It is striking that God didn't prevent the rabble from joining his people as they journeyed through the wilderness. He had a role even for them, which was ultimately to present his people with a choice—whether to trust God, or to listen to the voices that were making them anxious. So the rabble is actually is a symbol of freedom. We are free not to trust God. It is always an option for us to be perpetual complainers. It is especially striking that, when God got fed up with the people's complaining, he didn't just punish the rabble. No, everyone who listened to them was held responsible for their choice—and this is at least one reason why some churches are in so much trouble today.

Just as there is a rabble in every church, there is a rabble within every soul. Consequently, it is pointless to keep switching our memberships to different congregations, thinking that somewhere, somehow, we will find one that is rabble-free. We carry "the rabble" with us wherever we go. One of the most powerful reasons the dissenting voices within a church bother us is because we have yet to calm the dissent within our own souls. Even as we acknowledge its great flaws, the church helps us to see our own lives more clearly.

When we are ready to deal with this "rabble" within, we'll find that our only option is the one the Lord gave the Israelites. He never eliminated the rabble's voices from the holy community. Nor did he see the community as less holy just because it contained rabble. Neither are we less holy because there is both a believer and an unbeliever living within us. The point isn't to get rid of the dissent but to avoid being distracted by it.

The rabble confronts you with a momentous choice. Be sure to choose carefully, for there is something potently seductive about the voice that whispers, "You deserve better." Perhaps the smartest choice is to spend so much time listening to God that you have no time left for the rabble. It's the only way to move ahead on our own individual journeys, and clearly the only way for the community to move ahead on its way to the Promised Land.

There's a sign on the wall of my church office that declares, "You can't be the light of the world without attracting a few bugs." It hangs right next to the light switch, so it's the last thing I see at the end of the day when I turn off the lights. The sign is helpful because it reminds me that, if the church is doing its job, certain people will not really understand what we are doing, and they may frequently misbehave. Nevertheless, they are here for the same reason I'm here: We are attracted to the light. Even if we could succeed in getting rid of all "the bugs," we would at that moment fail in being a church that is being used by the Holy Spirit to bring together into one body those who desperately need our Savior.

LEARNING TO SPEAK MULTICULTURALLY

Since Pentecost, the ability to speak in different languages has always been a mark of the Spirit-filled church. Of course, this means that if we are not speaking the language of those outside the church, we are not being the church that the Spirit created. This task seems simple enough, but it is hard to do.

I started studying foreign languages in the seventh grade and continued throughout the course of my Ph.D. program. Learning a new language was never easy for me: Spanish, French, Greek, Hebrew—they are all difficult. In graduate school, I took the German exam five times before passing it. The real difficulty is not in poring over irregular verbs and vocabulary cards, or even in doing translations. No, the real struggle comes in learning how to think in another language, how to move outside of yourself and speak in other thought forms. But we as those who constitute the church have to do it.

Learning to speak in other languages is critical for effective ministry in our increasingly multicultural society. It is even more vital to our communication with friends and family members, for they all come from other family systems—which are cultures in themselves. When someone leaves one family in order to be married or even to befriend another person, a multicultural situation has been established. And at times, it seems as though we are speaking different languages.

How many times have you been in a heated conversation with someone when you could have sworn you were both speaking English, but you clearly were not communicating? You were not getting through to each other. You kept flunking the same argument. The problem is that you kept expecting the other person to understand you, while the other person kept expecting you to understand him or her. Neither of you could get beyond your own need to be understood—so you became lost in the argument, unable to communicate.

When I was a college student, I boarded a train in Paris, France, one night that was scheduled to take me to Geneva, Switzerland. I did not realize, however, that just because the whole train leaves Paris it does not mean that the whole train goes to Geneva. Along the way different cars are separated from the train and sent to other places. They announce all of this in French, but, as you already know, I have some difficulty with languages. Ignoring the strange words coming over the intercom, I fell asleep on the train, dreaming of Geneva. In the middle of the night, a conductor woke me up to tell me it was the end of the line. I stepped off the train with no idea where I was. Clearly it wasn't Geneva. It was just somewhere in Europe, I think. The station was closed. There was no sign on the platform. It was dark, cold, and snowing. I was completely lost and definitely frightened.

Whenever I talk to married couples who are having trouble communicating, I think about that night in Europe. These marriages invariably started out fine, with wonderful shared dreams about where they were going. But somewhere along the way things broke apart. Why? Often it was because they stopped listening to the "foreign language" the other person was speaking. Now they are feeling frightened, lost in a wintry loneliness. And they wonder how they got there—and how they can get out.

The essence of communication is to establish a *communion* between you and another. But you will not be able to do that unless you give yourself to another, and you will not be able to do that until you give yourself to the Holy Spirit.

Here again is another reason why it is so important to regularly find ourselves celebrating the Lord's Supper together with our fellow members. In the broken body and poured-out blood, Jesus provides the ultimate act of giving, as he establishes communion with us. It is an expression of love that is foreign to our normal way of operating, which is known not for its ability to give, but for its tendency to take all we can in a desperate effort to have our own thirst met.

The best communicating doesn't even require words. It just requires love. But you cannot give love unless you have received it. Thus we gather at the "family table" to tell the story of how much we are loved. In taking the broken body and poured-out blood of Jesus into our lives, we are renewed in God's passion for us, and we become able to communicate love to those who are lost in their needs.

When the next train approached that snowy platform on which I waited all alone, I jumped on it. I had no idea where it was going, but it had to be a better place than where I was. It was still late at night. The conductor whispered to me that we were heading for Italy; the train was packed, but he knew where one seat was left. He ushered me to the middle seat of a compartment filled with sleeping people. When morning came, I discovered I was sitting in the middle of an Italian family. We tried speaking to each other, but we didn't know each other's language. So we just sat there and smiled at each other for a while.

Before long, the mother said something to the son, who stood up and pulled a huge suitcase from the rack above us. She opened the suitcase, which was filled with food and wine. She shook open the tablecloth and spread it over our laps. Sitting in the middle of this I tried to look as small and inconspicuous as possible, but it was pointless. I was now part of this family. As the food went by, they kept insisting that I *mange* ("eat") along with them. And thus a little communion was shared between a family and a lost stranger. When we finally arrived at Milan, they all piled out of the train, dragging me with them, and they convinced the conductor to take our picture with me still right there in the middle.

So, also, every time we come to the Lord's Table we get another picture of what God has in mind for the whole world. His is a table at which there are no strangers. There is room, and grace, for us all.

WHO IS YOUR NEIGHBOR?

Jesus and a lawyer once engaged in a fascinating discussion about the necessity of loving both God and one's neighbor.[12] Seeking to avoid the real issue, the lawyer asked Jesus for a legal definition of *neighbor*. In response, Jesus told a story about a man on a journey who fell into the hands of robbers. They stripped him, beat him, and left him half dead. First a priest passed him by, then a Levite. Next came a man from Samaria, which was known as a place where "sinners" lived. Remember—the Samaritans and Jews were anything but good neighbors to each other. But the Samaritan took care of the beaten man. Then Jesus asked the lawyer who he thought was a neighbor to the man who had fallen into the hands of the robbers?

Notice Jesus' twist. The lawyer's question, "Who is my neighbor?" has been taken away from him and given to the man who was lying, bleeding and bruised, on the road. "Who is *his* neighbor?" Who belongs alongside him? In this parable we dare not identify with the priest or the Levite, and we probably cannot identify with the good Samaritan. The person we must identify with is the one who is in need of mercy.

The divided communities of our society clump us according to our similarities. Rich folks here, poor folks there. People of this color here, and people of that color there. Righteous people here, and everyone else way over there. Over against these divisions stands the neighborhood of God, which only has one group of people—those in need of mercy. The Samaritan could care for the beaten man only because he knew he himself was in need of mercy. And so it is with us. We take our place in the community of believers because we need to be there. It's the place that nurtures our thirst for holiness and points us to the Spirit.

When we drink in the living water of the Spirit in this community, we discover we cannot hide there. For the Spirit will always draw us to Jesus Christ, who refuses to stay in any one spiritual community. As Jesus himself declared, "The Son of Man came to seek out and to save the lost."[13] This is one of the reasons Jesus was killed in the first place. He kept refusing to stay within the borders of holiness constructed by the religious leaders. Throughout his ministry he kept confounding the people's understanding of holiness by loving the prostitutes and the tax collectors—those who were ignored and despised by the religious folk of that day. We have always been offended that Jesus' standards for maintaining holiness never seemed to be as high as ours. But Jesus was only doing the will of his Father, who will not allow his holiness to be contained by the religious. Every time we try to do this, whatever it is we are holding on to ceases to be holy.

Just as Jesus relentlessly sought out the unholy during his earthly ministry and made them holy by his presence, so also does he now reign over all the earth as the ascended Son who sits at the right hand of his Father. There is not one godforsaken corner of the world that is beyond his saving reach—which means, of course, that there is not one godforsaken corner at all. So when we come into the holy community to have our vision of this Savior renewed, we find ourselves compelled to leave with him, as he now, through his Spirit, roams the earth in search of the lost. We do not leave the church building to take Christ to the world, as though the world were void of Christ's presence until we arrive with him in tow. We leave with eyes that have been trained in worship to look for him out in the world, where he is, most assuredly, at work. And if Christ is there, the whole world can be seen as a holy neighborhood.

CHAPTER
12

FINDING A
HOLY PLACE

When we have finally found the well, that glorious place where Jesus gives us the living water of the Spirit, what we want most of all is to stay there. But staying in the place where it is easy to see Jesus is a prayer that is never granted.

WHERE IS JESUS STAYING?

One of the central themes of John's Gospel is that in Jesus we find the end to the soul's great search. This is why John devotes so many verses to describing Jesus' encounter with the woman at the well. He makes this same point in his opening chapter with a wonderful story about how two men discovered Jesus.

One day, when John the Baptist was standing with two of his disciples, Jesus passed by. John exclaimed, "Look, here is the Lamb of God!"[1] Hearing this, the two disciples left John and immediately began to follow Jesus. This response says a lot about both John and these two men.

What it says is this: They all knew John wasn't the answer to the soul's great search. John himself was particularly clear about that. His mission was to prepare the way for Jesus, and he realized that he wasn't the living water for anyone's parched soul. Neither is the church, the small group, or one's parent, pastor, mentor, or spiritual director. At their best, at their very best, these teachers of spirituality are only preparing the way for another.

The measure of our teachers is found in how graciously they let us leave them in order to undertake our search to find Jesus Christ. They will be able to do so only if they have not tried to make their students the solution to their own thirst. Only those who are clear about Jesus being their own Savior will avoid the temptation to be the savior for others.

We do not know how long these men had been following John. We do not know if they had followed someone else prior to John. What we do know is that as soon as John pointed to Jesus they immediately began to follow him. Maybe they recognized John's limitations; maybe John had been making his limitations perfectly clear. Whatever the cause, instead of trying to manipulate John into something that he was not, namely, living water, these two disciples left him to follow the true Savior, the only One who could lead them to such a sacred gift.

When Jesus noticed the two men following him, he turned and asked them what they were looking for.[2] Jesus didn't waste much time with chitchat. He always plunged right into the primary existential questions—questions that drive us during the course of our lives. *What are we looking for?*

I suspect there was a long pause after Jesus asked his question. It was the right question, the core question. It had led these men first to John, and then away from John. But it was a hard question. What *are* we looking for? Perhaps the two men looked at each other, then down at the ground, hoping the other would answer. Finally one of them replied, "Uh, we were just wondering, where are you staying?" What?! Confronted with the greatest, most pressing question of life, the best response they can come up with is, "Where are you staying"?

Actually, I find this easy to believe. Whenever Jesus asks me about my soul's insatiable thirst, I too usually respond by deflecting the issue. I ask him to help me write better sermons, get over a sickness, or have a nicer day. The real questions are just too powerful (maybe too painful even), and I have no answers that can stand up to them.

The fascinating thing about Jesus' response to their question is that he accepted their distraction centered around where he was staying: "Come and see."[3] So Jesus showed them where he was staying, and these men were never again the same. In the same way Jesus will put up with our petitions about relationships, health, work, and the many concerns of our daily life, but only in order that he might reveal more of himself to us through them.

We are told that it was about four o'clock in the afternoon when Jesus took these men home. It is very uncharacteristic of the Gospels to give such a precise time, so we're clued in here to something of importance. When we discover, at last, the place where Jesus is staying, it comes at a specific moment in the midst of our ordinary routines. True spirituality is not about trying to transcend the "dailyness" of this life, but about finding a Savior in the course of it. It can happen at four o'clock in the afternoon, at noon, or at two-thirty in the morning when you can't sleep and all you can do is wonder about what you're really looking for in life. The important thing is not when it happens but that you respond when it does. At some point, when Jesus "walks by" in your life, you have to choose to stay with him.

So these disciples weren't asking a dumb question at all. They were asking the question we all want to have answered: *Jesus, where are you staying? How do we find the holy place where you will offer us the water we are craving?* If we ask, he will show us.

THE COST OF ENTERING HOLY PLACES

Jesus will always invite us to the place where he is, but, as he warned his first disciples, the door leading into this holy place is narrow.[4] "Indeed," he later explained, "it is easier for a camel to go through the eye of a needle than for someone who is rich to enter the kingdom of God."[5] This was Jesus' response to the rich ruler who was saddened by Jesus' invitation to sell everything he owned and then follow him. The problem with being rich is that we have too many things in our hands and so much on our backs that we become bent over from the burden of it all. Because the door into the holy place is so narrow, we must let go of everything, absolutely everything, in order to slip through.

Some of us are rich in relationships. But there is no group ticket into the holy place. We must let go of our identities as sons and daughters, friends and lovers, in order to enter the lonely place where the Holy Spirit makes us the beloved of Jesus' Father.

Many are rich in wisdom. Some are even rich in theological knowledge. To enter the holy place, according to the apostle Paul, we must also drop all of our "wisdom" and become fools.[6] There is no way to add a little sophistication to this clear warning.

The powerful must become weak, the strong must become frail, and the successful must drop every achievement until they are no greater than those the world regards as failures. Those who have limped through life, hurt or angry, will finally have to let go of this as well. Skepticism, fear, sin, and even our own righteousness must fall from our hands—especially our righteousness. None of it will fit through the narrow door. Then at last, stripped of everything, we can encounter Jesus and his invitation to come to the holy place where living water is waiting for us.

Why does it cost so much to enter this holy place? Because we cannot see that the place is holy until we see Jesus there. If there is anything, anything at all, in our hands, it will distract us from seeing our Savior. But once we see the Savior, we will then see that all the things we have dropped are now in his hands, which, of course, is the best place for them to be.

From all the historical records we have of the early church, it appears that they celebrated Communion every Sunday. The most commonly used liturgy began with the leader saying, "The Lord be with you," to which the congregation responded, "and also with you." Then the leader would declare, "Lift up your hearts!" and the congregation would reply, "We lift them up to the Lord." During this time the church was often persecuted for the treasonous act of refusing to call Caesar their lord. Christians were excluded from certain professions, and often their property was confiscated. Sometimes the persecution was severe, even fatal. They never really knew who was going to be around for next week's worship service. But what were the most consistently spoken words in early church worship? *The Lord is with you, so lift up your hearts.*

In spite of all the hardship, loss, and persecution, the church was not discouraged. Why not? Because they knew that when they joined the church they were now united with Christ in his death. These words were woven into every adult baptism administered in the early church. To die with Christ meant they were dying to every other mission in life, every right, every relationship, and every piece of property. It could even mean they would experience literal death. Yet, because they had already died, they were no longer afraid of anything. After all, what could be taken away from them after they had already lost their lives with Christ? Better yet, because they had given up everything, and nothing now stood in the way, they were able to see that the Lord was with them. And having seen this, their places of worship, the catacombs and houses into which they would crowd, were revered as holy ground. They could not help but lift up their hearts.

I have watched the same thing happen in the waiting rooms of hospitals. While the life of a loved one is hanging on by a thread, the family is engaged in a struggle for their spiritual lives in the waiting room. As the pastor, it is my honor to wait alongside them. At first we talk, read Scripture, and pray. But mostly what you do in a waiting room is, well, wait. After we have pretty much run out of words and are sitting together in silence, God's Spirit begins a wonderful ministry. I've seen it many times. Uttering sighs that are too deep for human words to express, the Spirit prays on their behalf.

You first see the turning point in their eyes, then they break the heavy silence by saying, "Pastor, I can't explain why, but I know everything is going to be okay." Just to test things a bit, I ask, "The surgery is going to be a success?" "No," they respond, "I just know the Lord is with us." There it is! The little room littered with old magazines and half-empty coffee cups has just been transformed into the Holy of Holies.

HOLINESS IN TRANSIT

Several years ago my wife, Annie, and I visited some of our church's mission partners in the Holy Land. While in Bethlehem, we went to see the Church of the Nativity. After walking down underneath the church, we viewed the place where some people are absolutely positive Jesus was born. They even have a silver star right on the spot. The exact spot!

The star sits on a stone floor that is raised higher than the other places in the crypt. When the guide began to point out something at the opposite side of the room, Annie, who was at the back of the crowd, couldn't see him. In order to get a better view, but failing to look carefully around her, she stepped up on the raised stone floor and put her foot right on the silver star. An elderly orthodox priest went berserk at this point and screamed out the only English words he knew: "Holy place! Holy place!" Thinking she had created an international incident, Annie apologized profusely, but the priest just shooed us away from his holy place.

Such preoccupation with a silver star is hard for most of us to understand. But I wonder if we don't live with some of the same assumptions about holiness. Many of us have a place, or are looking for a place, we can call holy ground. For some it is a church sanctuary; for others it is a retreat center or a special place in nature. For still others it is a place from their past.

The church in which I grew up worshiped in a small, white framed building. It only seated about seventy-five people, and it was old and falling apart. My father, who was both pastor and janitor, held the place together with prayer and duct tape. But I still get misty-eyed when I think about that little white church. It was the place where I remember first hearing the gospel my father preached. It was where I was baptized and received Communion for the first time, where I as a young teenager stumbled my way through a testimony of my faith, and where I first heard missionaries tell us amazing stories about ministry in the Amazon. It was also the place where I first held the hand of the cute girl with daisies in her braids who later agreed to become my wife. (This was before she grew up to become the Great Desecrator of Bethlehem.)

Eventually we outgrew this little white church and built a new brick building that could hold hundreds of people. But those of us who had holy memories of the old place observed that things were really never again the same. Lots of room was made for new people to come and hear the gospel. Everybody raved about the wonderful ministry we were having. Still, the old-timers would say, "Yeah, but you should have been in the little white building. *That* was when we had church here." You would have thought the old church sheltered a silver star on the spot where Jesus was born.

Needless to say, this drove my father nuts. The thing I remember him saying over and over was that the point of a holy place was not to stay there but to carry the holiness away with you.

When the apostle Peter began his first letter to Christians scattered throughout Asia Minor, he addressed it to the "exiles of the Dispersion."[7] The last time we heard of "exiles" in the Bible it referred to the Israelites who had been carried into captivity to Babylon—which was not where they wanted to be. They longed for Jerusalem, the Holy City. Babylon, they thought, was a profane place, a place void of holy ground. Because they weren't in their old Holy City, the Jews found it difficult even to worship. Psalm 137 was written during this period of exile, and it captures quite eloquently the difficulty the Hebrews had in exercising spirituality during this period:

> By the rivers of Babylon—
> > there we sat down and there we wept
> > when we remembered Zion.
> On the willows there
> > we hung up our harps.
> For there our captors
> > asked us for songs,
> and our tormentors asked for mirth, saying,
> > "Sing us one of the songs of Zion!"
> How could we sing the LORD's song
> > in a foreign land?[8]

It's difficult to worship when we are in a place that does not feel holy. It's exactly what the members of the early church experienced when Peter wrote to them. These young, struggling congregations were surrounded by mystery cults and idolatry, hedonism and greed. Their cities were anything but sacred. They were like exiles living and working in unholy Babylon.

Life in our cities does not feel very holy either. Our days are jammed with making money and making the grade; receiving and sending faxes, answering ringing telephones, and standing by copiers that never seem to work. There are planes to catch, clients to call, reports to write, and deals to close; we concern ourselves with car pools and trips to the vet, the grocery store, and the dry cleaners. As we hustle from one thing to the next there is always some fool behind us honking his horn because we are in his way— and all of it wears down our souls, one small, steady drip at a time.

No one in Babylon is interested in helping us pray. How can we possibly sing the Lord's song in a place where holiness is so foreign? So we search for a place that feels holy in order to go there and be holy again.

In Old Testament times there were definite places where people would go to withdraw from the world and be renewed in God's presence. They would go to mountaintops like Sinai, Horeb, and Carmel, where magnificent and terrifying theophanies took place. They would go to deserts, difficult places where faith alone kept them alive. They would go to the temple, where the high priest would enter the Holy of Holies to offer atonement for the sins of the people.

Every time the people encountered God, he commanded them to live righteous lives. So holiness, in Old Testament theology, was found in two ways: The first was by *proximity*—by drawing near to the God who could be found in this world; the other was by *obedience*—by living as God told his people to live. As we are reminded by the psalmist, "The earth, O LORD, is full of your steadfast love; teach me your statutes."[9] Here, as before, we find proximity in this reference to God's love and obedience in this call to live by his statutes.

When we get to the New Testament Gospels, we read that Jesus, the Son of God, goes to all the traditional Old Testament holy places. He went to a *mountain*, where he was transfigured; he went to the *wilderness*, where he was tempted; he went to the *temple*, which he cleansed.[10] But the striking thing about these accounts is that these places are not considered holy apart from Jesus, who now makes the places holy by his presence, as he does every ordinary place. The Gospels, therefore, establish a great reversal. No longer do people go to a place to be made holy. Now the place is made holy by the presence of Jesus Christ. For us holiness is found by our proximity to Jesus and by our faithful obedience in following him.

When we move to the New Testament Epistles, we discover the apostle Paul telling the church that, as the body of Christ on earth,

"God's temple is holy, and you are that temple."[11] Similarly, Peter says, "Like living stones, let yourselves be built into a spiritual house."[12] Since the Son of God has come to earth, the locale of holiness has shifted from a holy geography to the holy community of Christ. There is no more a holy temple; there is now only a holy community of those who draw near to Jesus and obey him.

So, as my father was fond of saying, it is the mission of the church to carry the holiness of Christ with us into every corner of the world. Or as Peter would say, if you're feeling like you're living and working in Babylon, then be the living stones of holiness that the world will see.

MAKING THE PROFANE HOLY

While the Jews were locked in despair in Babylon, refusing to sing the Lord's song, the prophet Jeremiah gave them an inspiring word of hope. "For surely I know the plans I have for you, says the LORD, plans for your welfare and not for harm, to give you a future with hope."[13] This verse has been a treasure to people of faith for a long time. Like many, my wife and I have a copy of it hanging on one of the walls of our home. The hope and reassurance cascade into my heart every time I pass by this wall hanging.

But Jeremiah's prophecy also contains words that don't typically make it on a cross-stitch. Since the future belongs to God, the people were told to settle into the place where they were, for as long as they were there. They were instructed to "build houses and live in them; plant gardens and eat what they produce. Take wives and have sons and daughters." Then comes the real surprise: "Seek the welfare of the city where I have sent you into exile, and pray to the LORD on its behalf."[14]

If we really believe that the end of the story is filled with hope, we are set free from anxiety about today. We should even be so overwhelmed with gratitude for our hope that we can seek the welfare of those who have hurt us. So the point of hope is not to hang on until we get back to the holy place; the point is to be free to seek holiness in the place where we are.

We are accustomed to distinguishing between *holy* and *secular* as if they were opposites. But the concept of *secular,* which refers to things that are not holy, is a relatively new one. The Bible prefers the distinction of *holy* and *profane*. Since God created the earth, and all that is in it, everything is holy—as long as it points to the Creator. When we take things God created and pervert them for our own pleasure, we profane that which was given for a sacred purpose. For example, sexual intercourse within the covenant of marriage is holy, almost sacramental, but outside of marriage it becomes profaned. When money is managed by good stewards, it is holy; when it is hoarded or stolen from God, it too is profaned.

This truth also applies to workplaces and cities. We may think we work in Babylon, but our workplace is not outside God's holy creation. When we seek the welfare of the place where God has sent us, and "pray to the LORD on its behalf," as we have been commanded, this "profaned" place is restored to holiness.

This is the mission of the church, and its members are fulfilling it every day in small but profound ways. Take Ted, for example, who recently told me that he had been stuck for years in a terrible lawsuit that was going nowhere. All his efforts to settle the suit were fruitless. So he prayed not only about this legal mess but also for his opponents in the suit. Then, at the next meeting, he surprised those across the table by suggesting that they send to charity the settlement he had been seeking. They were so shocked that he didn't want the money, all they could say was, "Well, okay." At that moment, their bargaining table was on holy ground. They might as well have taken off their shoes and sung the doxology. How did that happen? Only because a businessman paid attention to his calling to seek holiness in the uncomfortable place to which he had been sent.

The Holy Land isn't just around Jerusalem. The Holy Church isn't just in a sanctuary. It is where we live and work. It is where we, the body of Christ, go day after day. It is where we do all the ordinary things as extraordinary acts of faithfulness to the God who led us there.

DON'T LOOK BACK

According to Luke, eventually there came a definite, specific moment when Jesus finished his ministry in Galilee and "set his face to go to Jerusalem." Just a few verses later we read, "As they were going along the road, someone said to him . . ."[15] All four of

the Gospel writers love to use that phrase and do so frequently—
as Jesus was walking along, something happened. Our encounters with
Jesus always occur along the way in life. Paul was on his way to
Damascus when Jesus encountered him; James and John were on
their way to go fishing; the Samaritan woman was on her way to
a well.[16] Ordinary people, like you and me, doing ordinary things,
but along the way they encountered Jesus—and nothing was ever
ordinary again.

Jesus can find us while we are on the way to the top or the
bottom; on the way to a great career or a terrible divorce. He can
find us on the way to our first apartment or on the way to a nursing home; on the way to give birth or on the way to bury the dead.
We may believe we were on the road up or on the road down, but
once we start following Jesus along the way in life, we discover
that we're always on the road to Jerusalem.

The Bible makes several things painfully clear about the road
to Jerusalem. It tells us, for example, that we are not there yet and
that we must keep moving. "As they were going along the road,
someone said to him, 'I will follow you wherever you go.'"[17] How
does Jesus respond to this great affirmation of faith? He cautions
the would-be follower, "Oh, but I have no place to lay my head,
no place to settle down." This reality is one of the hardest things
about following Jesus: He never settles down—which means his
followers never have a very settled life.

Have you ever been at a place where you had gotten your life
just right? You had close friends, a wonderful home, a healthy
family, enjoyable work, *and* a good church in which they sang
hymns you actually knew. Didn't you want to freeze the moment
by saying, "This is it. This is just right. Nobody move!" Well, quick,
take a picture, because this is always the moment when Jesus
blows a whistle and says, "Okay, everybody out of the pool." Jesus
didn't build a lot of houses; he didn't join a lot of clubs or churches.
He just kept walking toward Jerusalem. And if we are going to follow him, our lives are going to keep moving around on us.

Now, why is that? Why must we keep saying good-bye to
people we love? Why must we keep growing and changing and
maturing? Why do we have to keep losing things along the way—
our health, our families, and our dreams? Why can't we all just

stay right where we are? *What is so special about Jerusalem?* Most of
the time, Jesus' followers do not know.

Jerusalem is not merely an ancient city. In the Bible it stands
as a symbol of the ultimate holy place where our salvation is fully
manifested. It's the one place where we will finally understand
what Jesus is up to. In Revelation we are told about a new
Jerusalem to which all of creation is heading. It is the place in time
when God's reign is obvious, when creation is restored, and when
there are no more tears, no more pain.[18] Total and complete holiness on the new earth.

But we are not there yet. The new Jerusalem comes at the end
of the story. So, for now, we will always be clearer about what Jesus
is asking us to give up than about where he is taking us. Along the
way to Jerusalem, Jesus may take us places where we would rather
not go. He may bring gifts into our lives we would rather not have.
Each year of our lives, he will invite us to drop some of the things
we are carrying, because these things are becoming too heavy. They
weigh us down, and we're holding them too tightly. Jesus does all
of this simply to get us into holy Jerusalem, where our salvation
will become clear. By all means, Jesus cautions, don't look back. It
will only make the journey harder.

One of the greatest temptations to look back comes from all
the hurt we have left behind, hurt that still screams for our attention. Maybe it is hurt we caused; perhaps it is hurt someone else
caused. Or it may be a hurt caused simply by the volatility of life.

Barbara Kingsolver's *The Poisonwood Bible* is a preachy novel
(and even as a preacher I grew weary of it), but it has some good
moments. It pictures quite poignantly this last kind of hurt. It's the
story of a missionary family in the Congo torn apart by the fanati-
cism of the father, the violence of revolution, and the tragic death
of the youngest daughter, Ruth May, who was bitten by a ven-
omous snake. Everyone in the family is haunted most of all by little Ruth May's untimely death. In time, anger and guilt
overwhelm one of her older sisters, who feels responsible for what
happened. Near the end of the book, as the eldest daughter grows
older, she realizes she has continued to carry Ruth May "piggy-
back" since she died. She thought it was the only way to keep her
little sister near. But now as a mother herself, she knows this bur-

den has made it hard to care for her own family. There is a reason why we bury our dead. It is, after all, a way of placing them into the arms of God so he can carry them and we can move on.

Another reason people look back is because they like the past much better than the present. Have you ever noticed that the past always gets better with time? It seems to grow in value by mythic proportions. Recently my family returned to Long Island, where Annie and I had grown up. We drove by the old parsonage of the church my father pastored. I created a lot of wonderful memories in that great big beautiful house. I hadn't seen it in twenty-five years. It's a lot smaller than I remembered it being, and it needs work—a lot of work. When I mentioned this to Annie's mother, who still lives nearby, she said, "No, it looks pretty much the way it always has." But there it sat—an old, broken-down reminder that this was "home no more." It made me thankful that a day had come when Jesus called out, "Follow me. I have a lot better things to show you than this." At the time I was scared to leave. Now, I am so thankful.

There are many reasons we wish to turn back. One would-be follower wanted to bury his father. Another just hoped to say good-bye to his family. But Jesus' words are sharp, saying, "Let the dead bury their own dead. As for you, put your hand to the plow and don't look back."[19]

Jesus is not telling us we cannot grieve our losses or remember the past. No one ever gets over the death of a family member, and if we don't grieve we won't be able to keep moving on. In addition, no one ever continues to learn without recalling the past to some extent. No, Jesus is not taking the past away from us— but he is making it painfully clear that *life* awaits us down the road. We must keep moving in order to get there, and allow him to hold the past for us in his loving hands.

It can be hard to leave behind the life we have enjoyed and to keep moving—unless we really can see Jesus along the way. That is why we go to worship, Sunday school classes, and Bible studies. It's why we learn to reach out to others with compassion and care—and why we put our hands to the plow and do the work we've been given to do today. It's all a way of seeing Jesus.

You've got to keep your eyes on him, or you will never make it to the Holy City.

CHAPTER

13

FINDING A
HOLY PURPOSE

Society has done a good job teaching us how to run. We run out the door in the morning, run the kids to school, and run to work, where we run through the jam-packed day full of appointments, projects, and piles of paper. If we can break away, we run to the health club, where we mount a treadmill and run nowhere (an unfortunate metaphor). Since we are running late, we run to pick up the kids, meet friends, or get to a PTA meeting. We run through dinner or grab a little carryout "fast food" because there simply isn't time to cook. We run through the housework and office work due to be done by tomorrow before finally dropping exhausted into bed. *Exhausted* is good, because the last thing we want to do is ask ourselves why we are running so hard through life.

Finally, after six days of nonstop running, on Sundays we run into the sanctuary, where the unforgivable takes place: We're forced to slow down. Worship has things such as preludes, prayers, and all those awkward silent periods. We impatiently want the pastors to get on with it, as though their job were to package a little spirituality on the run for us so we can check worship off our busy schedules.

THE FAMILY BUSINESS

There is a reason why churches don't have drive-up windows. All worship should be designed to create an atmosphere in which our tired souls can at last find rest in God. Then, once we are reassured we are in a safe place, we can at long last hear the hope-filled words of God. Maybe that hope will come in the music, the Scripture text, or the sermon; maybe it will come simply from hearing once again the words, "In Jesus Christ, you are forgiven." The same Spirit who inspired the writing of God's Word can inspire our hearing of it. Suddenly we remember what the fast-moving world makes us forget—that we can stop running because we are forgiven of our sins and failures. We are loved and cherished. We don't have to keep living like fugitives. But we haven't heard the whole message yet.

Worship also reminds us that we are not alone. The sanctuary is filled with people who are exhausted. There is no *them* in worship, just *us*. All of us have come in search of the same thing, namely, living water. In the church of Jesus Christ, we find ourselves worshiping alongside the very people we have been racing against all week: women and men, overworked employees and overstressed employers, people who live in large homes and people who rent back rooms, people who are hurt and the people who hurt them.

We don't discriminate in worship. We simply declare that we are all sinners. We are not there because we are doing so well, but because we are on the run, desperately looking for mercy. When we realize the reality that all of us, different though we may be, are in the same situation, then a new vision for our life together is found in the sanctuary.

It is the vision of God running to us. All of us.

It doesn't matter if this worship is being conducted in a cathedral or in a storefront church. The Holy Spirit, the living water, rushes to us in all these ordinary places, carrying us back to our extraordinary home—the heart of God. There we remember again that we share the beloved Son's relationship with his Father. But the Son also had a mission. So one of the primary functions of worship is to renew our identity as beloved sons and daughters who work for the "family business," a work that calls us to love the world we fled when we ran into worship.

SPIRITUALITY IS WORLDLY

After the woman at the well left Jesus to return to her community in Sychar, the disciples were left alone with Jesus. They were concerned that he eat something, but Jesus wanted to talk about his real food, which is his work on behalf of the Father. Thus he stated, "I sent you to reap that for which you did not labor. Others have labored, and you have entered into their labor."[1] This was another way of saying that we have inherited a mission that began before we showed up on the scene. Our mission is to labor for the same kingdom of God that the Holy Spirit anointed Jesus to proclaim. But first we must listen and accept what God tells us in worship.

Once, when Jesus returned to his hometown of Nazareth, he went to the synagogue on the Sabbath, where he was invited to read from the scroll of the prophet Isaiah. After finding the text he wanted, he read these words:

> The Spirit of the Lord is upon me,
>   because he has anointed me
>   to preach good news to the poor.
> He has sent me to proclaim release to the captives
>   and recovery of sight to the blind,
>   to let the oppressed go free,
> to proclaim the year of the Lord's favor.[2]

After handing the scroll back to the attendant, Jesus sat down and said, "Today this scripture has been fulfilled in your hearing." Luke reports that everyone was quite impressed by Jesus—so far. These townspeople had watched Jesus grow up and presumably recognized that there was something special about him. Perhaps they had hoped he would be the One Isaiah promised would come to do such wonderful things—but only for the Jews.

Jesus frequently got in trouble with his second sentences. True to form, he went on to remind the congregation in Nazareth of two rather embarrassing stories from their past. The first recounted the time God sent Elijah to care for a Gentile widow, even though many widows in Israel were starving as the result of a famine. The second story described the actions of Elisha, who led a Syrian captain to healing from leprosy but did not do so for any of the lepers in Israel.

Both of these stories were the kind of incidents that many Jews preferred to gloss over precisely because they were reminders of God's compassion for Gentiles. God pronounced a blessing on Abraham so that in the end all families on earth would be blessed through him.[3] But some of those families had been hard on the Jews over the years. By the time Jesus showed up, nearly every known empire had marched through the Promised Land. Some had carried the people away into captivity. In Jesus' day the Romans were exacting enormous taxes out of the people. The Jewish people fervently hoped that God would soon deliver them from the hands of these oppressors. The last thing they wanted to hear was that God was being merciful to their enemy, which by this time was pretty much the rest of the world.

When Jesus finished his stories, everyone who had formerly spoken well of him became so filled with rage that they tried to throw him off a cliff. Rather than allowing this to happen, he walked through their midst and continued on with his ministry.[4]

This image of Jesus passing through the midst of those who were angry at him expresses beautifully what sometimes has to happen in worship. The word we hear from God may not be the word we were expecting, certainly not the word we wanted. We wanted God to tell us that there is a way out of this world. Isn't this what so much of the spirituality agenda is about these days— finding some way to climb out of the world? It is also what a lot of evangelical worship is about. But biblical spirituality and worship can never be reduced to making sure that God will at least take care of us and our future in heaven. So, the Word of God passes through our midst, leaving us angry and disappointed.

The purpose of our insatiable thirst is not only to have it satisfied by worshiping in spirit and truth, but to restore our lives as a blessing for the families of the earth. Or, like Jesus, to pray that we too may be anointed by the Spirit to bring good news to the poor. Simply put, we must bring the world into our spirituality and maintain our spirituality for the sake of the world.

When we refuse to do this, God refuses to keep running toward us in worship or in our prayers. Eli was high priest during a hard time in the life of Israel.[5] It was also a hard time in his own life. His grown sons, who were to inherit his sacred vocation, had contempt for God. They stole from the offerings that people brought to worship, and they brought their loose living right into the doors of God's sanctuary. The thing that bothered God the most, however, was that Eli turned a blind eye to their sins and failed to restrain them. In fact, as Eli grew older his eyesight literally began to fail. There was a great deal in the land, and in his own house, that he couldn't see. Maybe he didn't want to see it; maybe it just hurt too much.

Like Eli, sometimes we would simply like to remain in the house of God and not look at the problems in our homes or hear the cries of the world around us. But we can't be open to God without also being open to the things that break his heart. In Eli's day, "the word of the LORD was rare . . . visions were not widespread."[6] Likewise, if we close our eyes and stop up our ears to the injustice in the world, it will be impossible to see any visions from God.

SPIRITUALITY IS PUBLIC

Many of the contemporary advocates of an escapist-leaning spirituality try to point to the monasticism of medieval times as their model. As an example, consider the renaissance of interest in the monks today. Authors frequently manipulate monastic literature into manuals containing techniques for praying our way out of the world. But the monks never entered the monastery to escape the world. Rather, they carried the world with them in their prayers and sought to change society by placing it back into the transforming hands of God.

From the beginning, this has also been the agenda of liturgical worship in church. All the earliest churches had some type of liturgy they followed in their worship services. Many of these have been preserved, and they are in fact quite similar to the liturgies of churches today. It is noteworthy that the earliest churches chose to speak about their worship service as a *liturgy*. The word in the Greek *(leitourgia)* is derived from a combination of two words—*laos*, meaning "people" or "public," and *ergon*, which means "work." So *liturgy* refers to the public work of the people before God.

Before these words were "baptized" by the church, they had common, ordinary meanings. In Hellenistic society, when people built roads, entered military service, or served others in different ways, they were doing what was considered *liturgy,* that is, public work. So when those who did not go to church, or even have the slightest inkling what church was all about, heard the members of the church referring to their worship service as liturgy, they at least knew that Christians were worshiping God for the sake of all the people.

There was another word available to the early church to describe what happened in their worship services—a word that was completely rejected as inappropriate. This word was *orgia.* It was used to describe the private ceremonial rituals of those in the pagan mystery cults. Obviously, it is from this word we derive *orgy.* It is a sad commentary that many contemporary forms of Christian worship have abandoned the notion of liturgy, choosing instead to offer something resembling a personal orgy with God. If all our music in worship is reduced to songs that say little more than "Jesus is my boyfriend, and he really, really, really loves me," then we are hardly worshiping in spirit and truth.

Of equal concern are the churches that offer very ornate liturgy that is preoccupied with inaccessible symbols, words, and music. The liturgy is supposed to be a public work, and when we exclude the public, we are missing the point. It doesn't matter how eloquently we dress up the clergy or how many "insider" phrases the congregation learns to drone back, the question still remains, how is this worship helping to transform the world?

The purpose of worship is not outreach or evangelism; its purpose is to glorify God. So I have never been completely convinced by those who force every decision about their worship life to revolve around "accessibility" issues. However, regardless of the form, or liturgy, that is chosen, we must always bring the world with us into our Sunday services, just as we do in our daily prayers. This may even be the best evangelism we can offer the world, as we give it all back to God. We should pay no attention to those who tell us to bracket off the concerns of the world "so we can just worship the Lord." Before long, we'll simply end up as blind as old Eli.

SPIRITUALITY IS POLITICAL

At one point God became so fed up with the Israelites' refusal to live justly that he told them to just stop worshiping altogether:

I hate, I despise your festivals,
    and I take no delight in your solemn assemblies. . . .
Take away from me the noise of your songs;
    I will not listen to the melody of your harps.
But let justice roll down like waters,
    and righteousness like an ever-flowing stream.[7]

God has never tolerated worship inside his house unless his people pursued justice outside of it. Why? Because worship, prayer, and spirituality have always been the meeting places where heaven and earth come together.

It is more than a little significant that Jesus was killed as a political prisoner. Pilate even had a sign placed over his head that called him "the King of the Jews."[8] Indeed, the governor was more right than he knew. Jesus was not a king in the sense Pilate thought, but Jesus clearly claimed that he was bringing the kingdom of God to us. This reality is what he was talking about in Nazareth. In God's kingdom, there is good news for the poor, freedom for the captives, and recovery of sight for the blind—and there are no national boundaries. For us to accept citizenship in this new kingdom means we must also accept a whole new understanding of the norms of good citizenship. No one is ever abandoned in the politics of God's kingdom.

Some preachers assume that *preaching God's kingdom* means they must offer a political program for how to bring our society in closer harmony with the reign of God. I have never been impressed by these sermons and avoid giving them. Every Sunday in my congregation some of the nation's leaders join us in worship. They don't need to hear my opinion regarding what we should do about the defense budget. The reason they come to church is to hear a transcendent word from God—a word that can never be reduced to a mere political process. They come to have their vision renewed, to remember why they thought politics was a good idea in the first place, and to rekindle their hope that God has not abandoned the world to the politicians.

From both ends of the theological spectrum, we have witnessed the failure of churches to "legislate in" the kingdom of God. In the 1960s and 1970s the liberals were opening offices in Washington. In the 1980s and 1990s the conservatives followed the same course.

While their political agendas were dramatically different, their methods were essentially the same. They pulled from Scripture a vision of what they thought society should look like, then rushed to political processes to try to accomplish their goals. Now it has become clear to most of the leaders of these movements that they had to sacrifice too much of the gospel in order to fit it into a political agenda. This is not to say that a politician cannot be theologically motivated (many of them, in fact, are), but it is to say that there is so much more power to be found as we stand before almighty God than as we stand too long in the waiting room of a senator.

So, although worship has to be political in the sense of bringing the public with us as we stand before God, it dare not be political in the sense of reducing the church to a platform in the prevailing debates. For example, during the impeachment hearings of President Bill Clinton, I received a phone call from one of the network news anchors asking me if I was planning to call for the head of the president, or maybe for the head of the special prosecutor, at the upcoming Sunday service. I carefully explained that worship had higher purposes and that my calling was to bring the anxieties and anger of the people before the King of kings, who is more involved in our systems of government than we are able to see at the time. The voice on the phone responded, "That's nice, but it's a little too nuanced for the news." They would have to send their cameras somewhere else. The reality is, it may be as hard for our society to understand what we are doing in worship as it was for the society in the days of the early church. Still, it doesn't prevent us from ensuring that our worship keeps giving the world back to its only hope, its only Savior.

This is our purpose. It is why Jesus left us on this earth.

Spirituality Creates Leaders

Our society today longs for reasons to be hopeful. We enjoy unprecedented economic prosperity and more leisure time than we have ever known, but we still cannot find reasons to hope. Why not? Because hope comes not from making our lives more comfortable but from discovering great visions. The holy purpose behind making our way to the well where we can keep drinking in the living water is to discover these sacred visions for our life together.

Throughout history there have always been some men and women who are called to lead the way toward this hopeful future. These leaders are not born. They are created and shaped by worshiping communities who instill their great visions into young lives.

Of course, this assumes that the communities themselves are focused on God's visions. We do not change a society by starting with the leaders. In fact, God always started by calling aside a people who devoted themselves to digesting and inculcating his sacred ways of life. A historian recently summarized Lyndon Baines Johnson's presidency by saying he was not the best of presidents but, then again, we were not the best of peoples. We only get the leaders we create, and churches that know how to worship in spirit and truth are one of the best places in which to create leaders.

Where did Mother Teresa receive her vision to give dignity to the dying? Where did Martin Luther King Jr. get his vision of a color-blind society? Where did Frederick Douglass and Harriet Tubman receive their holy intolerance of slavery? From the churches that helped to shape them. When the abolitionist Sojourner Truth learned that the Ohio meeting hall she was scheduled to speak in had been burned to the ground by Southern sympathizers, she said, "Let them burn it, and I will speak upon the ashes!" She learned this kind of leadership from the Bible stories she heard as a child in her African-American church.

Churches create these kinds of leaders in a thousand different ways, most of which are impossible to chronicle. Churches can't simply put young men and women in front of crowds and expect them to lead. The church itself must set before its young people great heavenly visions. In youth groups today all across the world, teenagers are being confronted with a holy purpose for their lives.

When I was a teenager, quite a few youth groups experimented with coffeehouses. Ours was called *Agape*. (We thought it was a pretty cool name, never realizing that it was shared by half the church coffeehouses in America.) Every Friday night a ragtag group of us would drift into our church's annex. We would sit around giant wooden spools that had once held telephone wire but were now turned on their sides to serve as tables. The decorations were minimalist, each table adorned with but a single red glass candle with white netting around it. A skinny, middle-aged guy in tight jeans named Buddy was in charge—sort of. None of us really knew what he did for a living. We just knew he was always there, which was more than a lot of us could say about our parents.

After enough teenagers had gathered, Buddy would pull out his guitar and start singing. Sometimes he sang by himself, and sometimes he got all of us singing. "Michael, Row Your Boat Ashore," was a favorite, as were "Do Lord," "Pass It On," and "Amazing Grace" sung to the tune of "The House of the Rising Sun." At the Agape Coffeehouse we were always welcome to sing something of our own, or even to say a few words about Jesus, the Vietnam War, or our need for prayer because finals were coming up and we just weren't ready.

At the end of all this "sharing," Buddy would sing something really tender and then start talking about the most important things in the world. I don't remember a thing he said, but I do remember that it was he who said it. And that's why it was really important. I'm sure that what he was telling us was the very same thing my preacher-father was saying in "big church" across the driveway. But it takes a number of different voices to really declare the gospel so we can hear it. Teenagers need to hear it from someone who knows how to hang out.

Young Life, a ministry to teenagers, has always understood this and has served the church in extraordinary ways by helping kids understand the holy purpose to their lives—as have many other parachurch movements that came alongside the church as a different voice announcing the same things. When our national leaders on Capitol Hill give their testimonies, I frequently hear them mention their appreciation of a Young Life leader who was there at a critical time in their life.

God did not simply throw holy words down to us from heaven but allowed the Word to become incarnate, to become flesh, in Jesus Christ. So also do we mold the lives of young leaders, not just with our many right words, but by being God's incarnational witness to them. We spend time, and even waste time, with them. We

confront them, in their coming and going, with our own commitment to Jesus and his living water, the Holy Spirit. We cannot make
them believe, but we can at least make it clear that we believe.

As they come to believe, and continue struggling with unbelief, ever so slowly a holy purpose begins to shape their character.
It takes over their lives, and they know deep down that they were
created for sacred purposes. Then, someday, they will lead us closer
to God's hopeful future.

Spirituality Makes a Difference

As you can imagine, I attend quite a few funerals. The most moving part, typically, is the eulogy, when family members and friends
tearfully explain how this person had made such a difference in their
lives. In all of the funerals I have attended, no one has ever stood up
to celebrate how much money the deceased made. Never. Why not?
Because at the end of life we measure success not in wealth or power,
but in significance. We all hope that, when our own lives are over
and someone stands to give our eulogy, it will be said of us that we
lived a significant life—that we made a difference.

The best way to ensure that this eulogy is spoken is not to try
really hard to accomplish big things. Doing so just makes people
irritated with us. If big achievement is our goal, we'll run over
people on the way there, only to realize that our achievement
wasn't really big enough anyway. Ultimately, we'll only end up feeling both the sting of failure and the torment of intense loneliness.

Instead, let us follow the example of the Samaritan woman,
who brought people to the well where Jesus and his living water can
be found. Those who truly make a difference lead people to something bigger than any of us, something too sacred to be contained
by mere human achievements. We can't have a holy purpose unless
we are leading people to holiness, to "otherness," which means leading them to the One other than ourselves. When we consider the
men and women in the Bible and in the history of the church who
have made a difference, there are a few things that become clear:

We Must Choose Whose Side We Are On

From the moment Cain rose up to kill his brother Abel, the
world has been divided between those who do the hurting and

those who get hurt. When in history have we not known a struggle between taskmasters and slaves, greedy people and poor people, those who use people and those who love them? Paul called this the struggle between the children of darkness and the children of light.[9] Augustine called it the struggle between the cities of earth and the City of God.[10] Jesus called it the struggle between his Father and Satan.[11]

This is the great struggle that lies behind every war, broken home, scheming maneuver at the office, and piece of gossip we hear. If we are going to make a difference in this great struggle, we must first choose a side. If we keep returning to the well where Jesus can be found, he will force this choice on us. "Do not think that I have come to bring peace to the earth," he declared. "I have not come to bring peace, but a sword."[12] Jesus did not arrive as *God in the flesh* to make peace with this struggle. He never organized a summit for the Pharisees, the Romans, and the Zealots, where he asked, "Why can't we all just get along?" No, Jesus came to win the struggle, to defeat the evil that plagues the earth. Jesus entered our earthly struggles, claiming that these are all essentially struggles with God. Until we drink his living water and receive the Spirit who makes peace between us and God, we will never know which side of the struggle we are on.

How did Moses know which side of the struggle between the taskmasters and slaves to choose? Only by knowing and accepting his own identity as a Hebrew. Similarly, in the complex struggles we encounter every day, we will only know which side to take by accepting our identity in Jesus Christ. Only the Holy Spirit can bind us so closely to Christ that this identity becomes clear. But if we choose to accept this identity, we are also choosing to accept Jesus' struggle with the world. And when we do that, we cannot expect the world to treat us any better than it did him.

We Should Expect to Be Rejected by the Very People We Are Trying to Help

One day after killing a cruel Egyptian taskmaster, Moses tried to break up a fight between two Hebrews. Thinking he had performed his deed in secret, Moses was startled to hear one of them ask, "Who made you a ruler and judge over us? Do you mean to kill me as you killed the Egyptian?"[13] Moses realized that Pharaoh would hear about what he had done. Even worse, the people for whom he had sacrificed everything in his effort to make a difference did not want his leadership. So Moses fled to Midian, out in the Sinai desert.

This was a crushing blow to Moses. He eventually married and settled into his life in the desert. But for the next forty years he never got over the failure. When his first son was born, Moses named the boy Gershom, which means "an alien in a foreign land." I think it would have been tough to grow up as that kid. What a cruel name to give a son! Why would a father do that? Well, why do other parents mess up the lives of their kids? Because they have not recovered from their own hurts.

If you want to avoid being hurt or ever having to experience failure, avoid at all costs any attempts to make a difference. The saying is true, "No good deed goes unpunished." To make a difference is to introduce change—and people invariably resist the agents of change.

It is hard to find any good leader who did not face a great failure early in his or her life. After Paul was converted in Damascus, he tried to begin preaching there. The campaign went so badly he had to sneak out of town at night in a basket lowered through a hole in the city wall.[14] After beginning his ministry in St. Andrews, the Scottish Reformer John Knox was arrested and became a slave on a French galley ship. Jonathan Edwards, perhaps the greatest theologian our country has ever produced, was kicked out of the church he pastored in Northampton, Massachusetts. Medical doctor and missionary Albert Schweitzer was initially turned down by the Parish Mission Society because they thought he wouldn't make a good missionary.

Every parent has faced dark moments, thinking he or she was a failure in bringing up a child. Every spouse has had dark moments, thinking a marriage was not going to work. Everyone who has assumed leadership positions in government agencies in Washington, D.C., has experienced those same dark moments, thinking, "I should have never left home."

You tried to do something noble and right, but it didn't quite work out the way you had hoped. You've tried to put the failure behind you, but it is always there. You can't forget it. If you have children, you may be tempted to transfer all your dreams on to them now. If you do, you might just as well name your child "I'm a failure," because your earlier failure lies behind the pressure you are putting on your child. If you are alone, you might try simply to tend your own garden—but that won't provide much for your eulogizer to work with, will it?

The alternative is to use the wilderness to learn the lessons we can learn only there. It is in the wilderness moments that we discover how to let God make a difference in our own lives, and until God has made a difference in us, we cannot make a difference in the world.

We Cannot Make a Difference Until We Are Called to Do So

When the people rejected Moses by questioning who had made him a ruler over them, it was another way of saying, "Moses, you don't have the authority!" He really didn't. But after forty years in the wilderness with God, Moses was now called by God to lead the people out of slavery, and he was to do so with God's authority. Granted, it was still a struggle, but this time it was God's struggle.

Whenever we take on a holy struggle, whether in society or at work or home, it may appear obvious to us what needs to be done. But we need to remember that all struggles between good and evil are really between God and Satan. Paul explains, "We wrestle not against flesh and blood, but against principalities, against powers, against the rulers of the darkness of this world, against spiritual wickedness in high places."[15] If we think we are going to make a difference in a world plagued by the rulers of darkness without a clear calling from God, we are in for a painful surprise. We are in the deep end of the pool here. We cannot wade out into these waters unless we are sent by God. He is the only authority the rulers of darkness will respect.

It is striking how often we are told that when Jesus spoke, the people responded with amazement, because he taught them as "one having authority."[16] Where did Jesus' authority come from? Jesus did not go to seminary, nor was he ordained by a church. He was never elected to or hired for the job of being Messiah. No, his authority came from his Father. Even Jesus had to spend time in the wilderness before he began his great ministry.

It is only in the wilderness that we are spiritually prepared to make a difference. Spiritual preparation always takes time. We may think that we are ready, that we are trained and equipped to make a difference in some part of our world. But we aren't—unless we have done time in the wilderness, where we come to terms with our own thirst for God.

Our calling, our holy purpose, is not to get people out of the parched desert and into the Promised Land as quickly as possible. Nothing could be more dangerous for their souls. Our calling is simply to help them find the stream of living water along the way. But we won't receive that calling until—like Moses, Jesus, and everyone who has truly made a difference in this world—we first find in the desert refreshment for our own thirsty souls. What the people around us most need from us is to believe that *we* believe in the sacred river.

CHAPTER

14

FINDING A HOLY JOY

The ultimate purpose of spirituality is to fall deeply in love with God. It has nothing to do with how sophisticated we may become in prayer and everything to do with how passionate we are. When we make the goal of spirituality our own development, we preoccupy ourselves with measuring how far we have come—which is really only a preoccupation with how far we still have to go. But if our goal is to love God, we preoccupy ourselves with him and his sacred passions in the world around us.

LEARNING TO EXULT

When the woman at the well glimpsed who Jesus was and what his offer of living water meant, she ran back to town and with breathless excitement exclaimed, "Come and see a man who told me everything I have ever done! He cannot be the Messiah, can he?"[1] Having encountered Jesus along with this woman, we cannot help but run joyfully alongside her, echoing her excitement. We too have been found by One who knows us—who knows everything we have ever done—and yet mercifully still gives us the Holy Spirit, who makes us beloved sons and daughters of the Father.

It is enough to make you exult!

According to the dictionary, to *exult* means "to leap up with joy." So this is not the serene, everything-is-in-shambles-but-I'm-okay sense of joy we sometimes talk about. To exult is to be overwhelmed with more joy than our bodies can contain. We can't even stay seated, and we certainly aren't worried about preserving our dignity. When we experience this exulting type of joy, we simply must leap to our feet and scream, "Alleluia!"—or something like that.

When David contemplated God's strong hand of protection for him, he responded by praying, "I will exult and rejoice in your steadfast love."[2] We talk about this love of God in worship all the time, so why don't we see more exulting? Time and again we encounter the Word of God offering a sacred "I love you." How can anyone hear these amazing words and think, "I know God loves me. Why does the pastor keep saying that?" Imagine taking the risk of telling someone, "I love you," only to hear back, "Yeah, I know, I know." Yuck!

When we hear again and again that God loved us so much he sent his only begotten Son, we simply have to make some sort of response. We can preserve our dignity, I suppose, and quietly reassure ourselves that we know all about this. Or we can really get the message of the sacred "I love you"—and let it transform our lives. We'll know we've done so when we discover a little more bounce in our step because, well, we're in love.

According to the prophet Zephaniah, God is the One who started all this exulting. The venerable prophet began, however, by warning us about the dark day when God will appear on earth. It will be a time of angry judgment, since we have all turned back to our old idols. However, the jump from judgment to exulting is not far for God. Even his anger is rooted in his love. God loves us too much to allow us to continue wasting our lives at the feet of false idols who cannot save. So he comes and finds us. But if, like the woman at the well, we have a good memory of everything we have ever done, a visit from God will certainly seem like judgment.

But then a great reversal takes place. On his way to find us, we are told, God decided to set aside his judgment and to come to us with joy. He is so delighted simply to find us. Thus Zephaniah exhorts God's people to exult:

Sing aloud, O daughter Zion;
    shout, O Israel!
Rejoice and exult with all your heart,
    O daughter Jerusalem!
The LORD has taken away the judgments against you. . . .
The LORD, your God, is in your midst,
    a warrior who gives victory;
he will rejoice over you with gladness,
    he will renew you in his love;
he will exult over you with loud singing
    as on a day of festival.[3]

The real reason Christmas should be a festive holiday is because in the birth of Jesus, the Lord God came into our midst—and didn't kill us! If we are not absolutely overwhelmed by the Christmas story, we are not reading carefully enough.

Not only does God not judge us, he rejoices over us. So much joy does God have that he just has to start singing. Loudly. According to Zephaniah, God sings in exultation, which is the stand-up-and-really-let-er-rip kind of singing. Not even God can stay seated when Christ is born, because he is delirious with joy and love. We have been found!

To be found by God means more than just not being lost anymore. It means that we now have the opportunity to be restored to what God created us to be from the beginning. Because we have all spent too much time bowing down to idols, we have so corrupted God's image in our lives that, not only do we not know who *he* is, we don't even know who *we* are. Until we realize that we have been found in Jesus Christ, we will keep pretending to be so much less than we really are.

In India, the fable is told of a tiger cub who lost his mother and was adopted by a family of goats.[4] The goats raised the tiger to speak their language, adopt their ways, and eat their food. Soon the tiger believed he was just a funny-looking goat. One day a king tiger appeared, and all the goats scattered in fear. The young tiger was left alone, feeling afraid, yet somehow unafraid. The king tiger asked him what was meant by this masquerade. All the young tiger could do was bleat nervously and eat grass. So the king carried him to a pool and forced the young tiger to look at their reflected images. Side by side, the truth was made clear in what they saw mirrored in the water. Lashing his tail and digging his claws in the ground, the young beast finally raised his head high, and the jungle trembled at the sound of his exultant roar.

True spirituality will not help us cope with life as a goat or make us content with our own pieces of turf or dress us up as a Pharisee goat. No, true spirituality invites us to discover our true image in the king born among us.

He lived with us as one fully alive. Nothing escaped him in life. Not the dead sparrow, the children who tried to climb into his lap, or the woman who touched the hem of his clothes.[5] The lame, the blind, the hungry, the sinful—all these stirred his compassion and compelled him to reach out. He knew how to keep the party going at a wedding in Cana and how to weep at the death of his friend Lazarus.[6] He lived both at the heights and the depths of life and made every ordinary moment in between seem holy. He loved life but was willing to lay it down for the Father's love of the world.

The contrast between his sacred-human life and our goatlike lives is so great that we must either crucify the king tiger in order to remove the judgment his presence creates, or we must change. But how can we change? If Jesus is just an example, then he is a curse because the example is too great; we cannot follow it perfectly. But if he really is *God with us*, then in his arrival we are enabled to see the image of God in our own lives. As we embrace this Savior the divine image comes alive in our own hearts. Jesus restores our dignity by forgiving us for all those ways we have settled for being the goat, so that we can spend the rest of life expressing gratitude and roaring with delight.

Hot Faith

We can, of course, reject this hope, and we can certainly accept it and take it to heart. But God has always reserved his greatest judgment for those who remain indifferent—and who think God is indifferent. According to Zephaniah, what angers God most is the belief that "the LORD will not do good, nor will he do harm."[7] No matter how much we may think this is true, the Christmas miracle proclaims that God is passionate about us, and he expects us to respond with passion as well. Again, that is part of what it means to be made in his image. Since God is not indifferent, he cannot tolerate our indifference. He hates *lukewarm*.

Laodicea was once an impressive town. It was the kind of place that perpetually topped the polls as the best place to live in Asia Minor. Economically it was very well-off. By the end of the first century it boasted strong banking establishments and a successful textile industry. It even had something of a medical college that specialized in eye problems. The Roman historian Tacitus tells us that when a devastating earthquake struck in A.D. 60, the people of Laodicea just rebuilt the city with their own reserves, taking no aid from Rome. This city was in great shape. It was prosperous, educated, and on the cutting edge of technology.

Laodicea had just one small problem—it had lousy drinking water.

While the town was strategically located along a lucrative trade route, it wasn't near a natural supply of fresh water. The town architects thought they had solved the problem. From a town six miles to the south, they imported cold water through a stone aqueduct; from a town to the north, hot water flowed down from the natural hot springs. So they had hot and cold running water—or at least they were supposed to. Like many good engineering ideas, this one didn't quite work. The aqueduct developed cracks in time, which compromised its ability to insulate the cold water. By the time it arrived from the south, it had warmed up. And when the hot water arrived from the north, it had cooled down—which meant that all of the water in Laodicea had an awful lukewarmness to it.

When the Laodiceans discovered in John's Apocalypse, the book of Revelation, that the Lord called them lukewarm, they probably grimaced. He had hit them in their one soft spot. "I know your works," declared the Lord. "You are neither cold nor hot. I wish that you were either cold or hot. So, because you are lukewarm, and neither hot nor cold, I am about to spit you out of my mouth."[8] Remember, the people to whom Jesus was speaking were the members of the church. They weren't cold, and they weren't hot. They were lukewarm.

Imagine discovering that someone's commitment to you is lukewarm. Who wants that? It's a bit like taking a big gulp from a cup of coffee that has sat on the desk all day long. It just leaves an awful taste in your mouth. This is how Jesus characterized the Laodicean church's commitment to him. When he thought about it, he just started looking for a good place to throw up.

What went wrong? As with most relationships, things between Jesus and the Laodiceans didn't begin badly. Like the water that started out hot up north, the Laodicean church began with passionate faith, but along the way things had cooled down. In all probability, all of their wealth, commerce, medicine, education, and hard work to build a good life for themselves had distracted them from their passion for God, which in turn, distracted them from their passion for life.

Distraction is the great danger for the American church as well. The problem for the church in our culture today is not primarily that our teachers cannot pray out loud in school or that we cannot hang the Ten Commandments in our courts of law. Rather, the great problem is that we are too easily distracted by our resolve to get things exactly right—which has the effect of flattening out a human soul that was created for the heights and depths of life. We were not created to engineer our lives; we were created to live them.

We work so hard as we pursue excellence in our jobs and in our families, but we settle for a lukewarm, indifferent relationship with God. Who among us would miss a day of work because we are just too busy to go to the office? But how many days have we been too busy to read the Bible or to pray? Who would tolerate a relationship where we never talk? But don't we expect God to accept this kind of attitude from us? It isn't that we made a conscious choice to forget about our relationship with God. It's just that we got, well, distracted. We became too busy looking for ways to make improvements in life. And God? Well, we simply assume, "The LORD will not do good, nor will he do harm." Nothing could be more dangerous. Such spiritual apathy leaves the worst lukewarm taste in the mouth of a passionate God.

Not only were the citizens of Laodicea preoccupied with getting their city just right, they were also so prosperous that they couldn't see their need for a Savior. "You do not realize," says the Lord, "that you are wretched, pitiable, poor, blind, and naked."[9] It is striking that Jesus told a rich city that they were poor, a city known for its booming textile industry that they were naked, and a city known for its eye treatments that they were blind and could not see clearly.

I have never met anyone who admits to being rich. Even those who are rich according to certain objective standards don't think they have enough. We are all tempted to think that if we just had a little bit more money, we would be okay. The sad truth is, no matter how much money we accumulate, we always seem to "need" just a little bit more. The prophet Haggai was talking about most of us when he said, "You that earn wages earn wages to put them into a bag with holes."[10] No one is as poor as those who have wasted life collecting "a little more" money; no one is as blind as those who cannot see that life is a gift.

Why, then, would we let what we do not have define us? Every part of our lives is flawed. So what if the water isn't hot enough or cold enough? So what if a job isn't what we hoped it would be? Whose is? So what if life hasn't turned out the way we thought it would? These disappointments confront us with a key choice: We can waste every day of our lives fixing things that really don't matter, or we can give thanks.

Gratitude is a choice to live with a holy joy that cannot be diminished by our failures in "engineering." We find gratitude by realizing that even the flaws can become channels for the grace of a God who is passionate about us—just the way we are. When we finally discover this reality, we become irrepressibly passionate ourselves. Lord knows, Laodicea could use a few more people with passion.

RECKLESS ABANDON

When we were young, our parents repeatedly told us, "Be careful!" Apparently they said these words enough times to make them stick. We still hear the phrase every day, except now the words come from the backs of our minds: "Be careful!" But perhaps we overlearned this lesson. When it comes to things such as health and morality, being careful is pretty important, but there are other times when it is not as wise—like when we are trying to enter the kingdom of heaven.

Jesus once said the kingdom of heaven is like a man who sells everything to buy a single pearl.[11] Clearly, to do so is not "being careful." What could possibly make him so reckless? He would have to be certain that this one thing is more valuable than everything else—which is, after all, exactly the way we must come to God. Actually, it would be reckless to come to him carefully. We had best approach God with sheer abandon and place all of life into his hands.

Those who have given everything to God are free to live with increasing passion because they are no longer worried about losing things. They already lost it all when they came to God. Nor are they worried about making mistakes—and this sets them free to take remarkable risks. The last thing we want to do is to show up at the gates of heaven and declare, "I really don't need grace. I made no mistakes because I never risked giving away my life." This statement will not play well in heaven.

The Bible is filled with illustrations of people who made huge mistakes trying to do the right thing. Abraham, Moses, David, Peter, and Paul all made terrible mistakes. But their mistakes were easily redeemed by God, and their lives did not end in failure. By contrast, the servant who buried his single talent of money out of fear of losing it was thrown into the outer darkness, where there will be weeping and gnashing of teeth.[12] Apparently, in the strange economy of God, *failure* is defined as "breaking even." But when we take risks, we are living by faith, and God cares much more about the strength of our faith than he does about either our successes or our losses.

This truth supplies, in part, the reason we have been given the biblical doctrine of heaven. People who believe there is a heaven act differently than others. They make choices more easily because they recognize that these choices are seldom ultimate. They are less cautious in their approach to life, more likely to laugh at themselves, and a lot more likely to give themselves to others. They are able to do this because they don't waste much time trying to be their own savior. No one gets to heaven by being good enough; we get there only because Jesus Christ has prepared a place for us. Because of this reality, the woman at the well could return to the people who had scorned her, without caring about their judgments. What did she care about the condemnation of anyone on earth? She had just met the Messiah in whom heaven and earth come together.

We have been taught that our future is determined by the choices of our present—which makes us cautious and fearful. But the doctrine of heaven proclaims just the opposite. The end of our story is already written. By the grace of God it ends wonderfully. There's not a thing we can do to make it end any better. And because the ending is already written, we are free to enjoy the mystery of today without worrying about where life is heading. All we know about tomorrow is that Jesus is waiting for us, in life and in death.

"'I am the Alpha and the Omega,' says the Lord God, who is and who was and who is to come, the Almighty."[13] Therefore, history is not running amok. It began with the decisive act of God's creating. It has its decisive center in the advent of the Son of God. And it is moving toward the definitive future of what God alone has prepared, without our help. He is the Alpha and Omega, the beginning and end of our lives. These words were not written to resign us to a rigid determinism; they were meant to free us to live joyfully, with abandon, as if today is all we have—which, of course, it is.

In Saint Benedict's little rulebook for people living in monasteries, the sharpest criticism is reserved for complainers. Benedict even made it an offense worthy of excommunication—in part because a complainer can drain all the joy out of a community. More important, our complaining reveals a lack of faith. It assumes that current circumstances are more powerful than the Savior, who has not finished unfolding the sacred mystery of our lives.

So those of us who have been to the well and have tasted the living water need to repent of our pessimism. Without question, the present appears to be quite dark at times. But you don't have to have met Jesus in order to believe this. Go to the movies. Turn on your television. Read a best-selling novel. For the most part, the message you'll hear is that we have lost our way in the darkness. Nearly everyone recognizes this reality. If we really want to be prophetic, we need to say something useful. We need to remind people that we are not writing the story of our own lives—*God* is. So the future is never determined by the present; it is determined by the Lord God, "who is and who was and who is to come."

LAUGHING WITH GOD

Pastors are used to helping people keep on believing, even when bad things happen to them—but what about when good things happen? The truth is, it really isn't too difficult to cry with God; laughing with him feels much more foreign to us. An old couple from a city called Ur were among the first to learn this.

Abram was seventy-five years old when he began his journey with God; Sarai was ten years younger. But when God promised that if they only followed his dream he would bless them with family, land, mission, and, best of all, a future, they decided to take the deal. They left everything, believing that God could be trusted.[14]

Nearly a quarter of a century later, Abram and Sarai had wandered around more than they might have expected. They had enjoyed some good years and had survived some bad years. What they hadn't received were any babies.

It was Sarai who had originally come up with the idea of Abram having a baby with her slave-girl Hagar.[15] The child, named Ishmael, was now thirteen years old. Every time Abram and Sarai looked at him, they must have thought, *This isn't exactly what we dreamed about*—but then again, they must have decided, *It's just the way life is. Sometimes you have to settle.*

Then one day, out of the blue, when Abram was ninety-nine years old, God returned to speak to him again. As soon as Abram realized that it was God speaking, he fell on his face in worship. The first thing God did was introduce himself with a new name: *El Shaddai*, "God Almighty." Then God reaffirmed his earlier promise to Abram, declaring that he would make him "exceedingly numerous." Finally, God changed Abram's name to *Abraham*, which means "ancestor of a multitude of nations."[16] By now Abraham was standing back up; in fact, he was standing pretty tall. "Yes! I really will be the father of many nations. God will bless Ishmael.

The Almighty just needed a little help from me and, of course, Hagar."

This is how we often handle God's unbelievable promises to us, isn't it? We turn them into reasonable goals that we resolve to attain for ourselves. Having received the most extraordinary promises of blessing, we dilute them into our own ordinary achievements. Then when we come to church and hear the blessing reaffirmed, we assume that our busy, though unhappy, lives must be what God had in mind. It's not the blessing we had in mind, not exactly, but it's a reasonable settlement.

God doesn't settle so easily. Remember how the story goes? God still has something to say to Abraham, as he announces, "Oh, and I'm also changing Sarai's name to Sarah, because, don't forget, she and you are going to have a baby boy." Now Abraham falls down on his face again. Only this time it's because he is laughing too hard to keep standing up. "What! I am having a what? I was pretty impressed I had a son with that young thing Hagar when I was eighty-six, but this is ridiculous!" Actually, the words from the Bible are, "Can a child be born to a man who is a hundred years old? Can Sarah, who is ninety years old, bear a child?"[17]

The very first sermon I preached as a seminarian was on this text. Unfortunately, I gave it in a nursing home. I thought I was being relevant. Many of the residents were in wheelchairs, and most could barely hear me. But I went ahead and pointed out that Abraham and Sarah were older than most of them. "Imagine that," I remarked. "You can all still have babies!" Most of my listeners were not encouraged by this. One woman actually interrupted me and yelled, "Preposterous!" Well, at least she got the message right—this news *is* utterly preposterous.

After the sermon, the nursing home chaplain, a middle-aged woman, came up to talk with me. She said, "You know, I've always wanted a baby, but I'd given up hope. After your sermon I've decided to hope again." I immediately began to backpedal. "You know, I was *just* preaching. You must be realistic. A lot of people want babies and never get them." Sheesh.

My response to this woman certainly carried grains of truth in it. People do die even after we've prayed that they would be healed. Marriages do break apart in spite of spouses working hard at reconciliation. We don't always get the wonderful job we apply for. And in spite of all our prayers for the world, it is still marred by war and violence and starvation. Of course we do not always get what we really want—but that does not mean that we dare give up the joy of having hope.

We are a people who must have hope. Not just because it makes us feel good, but, more profoundly, because God is involved in this world. The most powerful illustration of this truth can be seen in his coming to be with us in Jesus Christ. After all we have seen Jesus do in his life on earth and in his death on the cross, after he rose from the dead, who knows what a risen Savior may do in our lives? Do we dare tell this Savior God to be realistic? God is the One who creates reality, and with God all things are possible.

Apparently, Abraham's encounter with God seemed so bizarre that he couldn't even share it with Sarah. A little later, when several angels came to remind Abraham that God was, in fact, serious about Sarah having a baby, she overheard them through the tent walls. This time it was Sarah who started laughing. In response, God asked Abraham, "Why did Sarah laugh? . . . Is anything too wonderful for the LORD?"[18]

This really is the question, isn't it? Those of us who have waited and waited for a blessing from the Lord, who have grown so weary of waiting that we have edited down our dreams, must face this question. Those who have settled for bodies that do not work very well, for loneliness that permeates the end of every exhausting day, or for jobs that strip away every shred of our passion—what would happen if one day out of the blue God were to say, "The waiting is over. It's time to recover your dreams"? Would we say, "Preposterous!" Or would holy joy well up again within our hearts, freeing us to say, "Why *not?* Is anything too wonderful for the Lord?" It all depends on what we have discovered about the Lord.

Our job is not to worry about when, or if, we will receive the desires of our hearts. That is up to God. Our job is to pray and to hope. And along the way, as we pray, we are drawn closer and closer to God. In time we will discover that being drawn close to God is even more important to us than our dream, because alongside God is where holy joy is found.

It is significant that God changes the names of Abraham and Sarah before they have a son. By doing so, God makes it clear that their identity is determined more by the promise than by the fulfillment of the promise. It is even more significant that God first reveals to them a new name for himself. He is *El Shaddai*—God Almighty. What could possibly be too hard for someone with a name like that? But until Abraham and Sarah discovered this truth, they would never discover hope in their own lives.

The same thing is true for us as well. There is infinitely more to God than we know, and until we discover more of this precious mystery, we will never find any mystery in our own lives. Where there is no mystery, there is no hope; and where there is no hope, there is no laughter.

We are given no indication that God bawled out Abraham and Sarah for laughing. In fact, he seems to join in the laughter by telling them to go ahead and name their son Isaac, which means "he laughs."[19] You have to believe that every time they looked at that kid, every time they called *He Laughs* to come in for dinner, they broke out in the biggest smiles. And they remembered, "Is anything too wonderful for the Lord?"

There is an important epilogue to the story. As promised, God blessed Isaac, but he also blessed Ishmael and promised to make him into a great nation.[20] Today the great Arab people of Ishmael and the great Jewish nation of Isaac are having a difficult time living together peacefully in the Middle East. Some would say, "They've never lived together in peace. They'll always be at war. That's just being realistic." But it's also realistic to say that they've both been blessed by God. So we continue to enjoy the dream, and we hope for and work toward the day when Ishmael and Isaac live together in Jerusalem as brothers. Is that preposterous?

It all depends on your vision of God. But remember, the last thing you ever want to tell God is to be realistic.

CHAPTER 15

FINDING A HOLY SELF

As we learn how to delight in God, we finally are enabled to delight also in our own lives. This is not *our* goal in spirituality; it is God's goal.

We nurture spirituality in our lives in order to share in the Son's passion for the Father. It's the reason we keep bringing our thirsty lives back to the well to drink in more of God's Holy Spirit. As we are filled with the Spirit, we begin to believe that God is also passionate about us.

No one really falls in love in order to be loved, but it certainly is a nice benefit. It's also the only way we can receive the lives we have been given.

THE FRIENDSHIP OF THE LORD

When we refer to God as *Father*, many of us think first of his high expectations for us. Why? Perhaps it's because the image of God we've had since childhood is one that stresses how much he has done for us and how little we have done for him. Falling short of expectations, we are told, makes Daddy very disappointed. This vision has the effect of making all our efforts at righteous living little more than a codependent striving to appease a father who can never be satisfied, no matter how good we may be. So even as adults we continue to be more afraid of God than in love with him.

The Bible does tell us to fear God, but not because of his high expectations. It tells us to fear his love. "The friendship of the Lord," King David explained, "is for those who fear him."[1] The Creator of heaven and earth demonstrated his great love for us in the passion of Christ on the cross. But this is no ordinary friend we have. He will certainly be hard to control. He will not tell us only those things we want to hear, show up only when we want him around, or be just another ornament in our neatly ordered lives. This friend will take us places we would rather not go and give us passion for things we would rather not have passion for. Hardest of all, God will enjoy us even when we are afraid we're not good enough to enjoy him, or ourselves for that matter. But this is what the life of the Son of God among us is fundamentally about.

We do not tend to picture Jesus as having friends, and we aren't inclined to think of the disciples as his friends. We think of them more as Jesus' bumbling students who could never understand exactly what he was saying or doing. But a few short hours before Jesus was arrested and crucified, he told them, "I do not call you servants any longer, because the servant does not know what the master is doing; but I have called you friends, because I have made known to you everything that I have heard from my Father."[2]

I wonder what was going through their minds. Were they surprised? Honored? My guess is that they were once again confused. We regard friends as peers, and although the disciples loved Jesus, they were hardly his peers. Neither are we. So it does mystify us to think that Jesus would one day identify us as his friends.

What does it take to become a friend of Jesus? Apparently it must involve more than serving him. Servants simply fulfill a job. They don't strive to understand the mind of their Lord, and they certainly don't maintain a loving relationship with him. They simply do their jobs.

Maybe we would prefer to remain servants. It's easier, clearer, and much less demanding. Friendship is frequently confusing and mysterious; it requires a great deal of trust, and it is all too easy to get burned along the way. But the greatest challenge in friendship is learning how to receive from someone else. You can't always give to or serve your friends. Eventually you have to let them serve you. This is exactly why we have a hard time thinking of ourselves as Jesus' friends—but only his friends find relief for their deep spiritual loneliness.

Until we believe that this Friend was honestly dying to love us, we will never think there is much worth loving in ourselves. Conversely, once we do believe we have this sacred Friend, we can set free our other friends and family members from trying to provide the well of love only a Savior can offer. Human hearts are simply not deep enough. But having freed our loved ones from the burden of being our savior, we can then delight in them as God's beautiful blessings in our lives.

BEHOLDING BEAUTY

Although I have officiated at hundreds of weddings over the course of my ministry, I still get choked up, usually during the vows. When the groom vows, "I will always be your loving and faithful husband," I look into the bride's eyes, and it is so obvious that she is buying it. She believes him. She expects him to keep his word and always be loving to her, just as he expects her to do when she makes her vow to him. It is so tender—and so naive—that it brings a tear to my eye every time.

I think to myself, *Certainly she knows this guy well enough to recognize that he is a mere mortal. He's going to hurt her, as she will him.* They may not actually commit adultery, but they will surely break these wedding vows in some way or other. Everyone does. In spite of saying the words in front of God and the congregation, no couple remains "always loving, always faithful." So what makes them think this relationship is going to work out?

If they are really clear about the love of God, then the basis of their marriage is not their vows, but God's vow. As Jesus promised, the Holy Spirit will come like rivers of living water flowing out of their hearts and coursing into the other's life.[3] The floodgate that opens these waters for us is our own belief. Jesus was quite specific in referring to the "believer's heart" when he made his promise. What we have to believe in is not the vow of the person we are marrying and certainly not our own vow, but God's promise to give us so much love that it will overflow into all our relationships.

One of the great benefits of receiving this living water is that, like a person madly in love, we begin to see the whole world differently. We are no longer disappointed in the world, because we aren't looking for something or someone in it to fill the emptiness within ourselves. Beauty can be seen, honored, and even adored— without having to possess it.

I will never forget the opportunity I had to sit in St. Peter's Basilica in Rome and stare at Michelangelo's amazing sculpture, the *Pieta*. I was lost in the graceful lines and contours that invited me into the tender pathos of Mary compassionately holding the lifeless body of her son on her knees. To say I enjoyed this work of art would be a great understatement. I sat there for over an hour, mesmerized, as the sculpture told me more about a mother's grief than I had ever imagined possible.

But it never occurred to me to say, "I must get one of these statues for my backyard." I don't need to own it or control it in order to adore it. The statue belongs to the church, and the church belongs to God. Not owning it doesn't prevent me from delighting in it. On the contrary, my ability to enjoy it is directly related to my ability to refrain from entertaining fantasies about owning it.

Relationships don't belong to us either. They too are the artwork of God. Most of the time when a relationship runs into trouble it's because someone has tried to control the art. Because we are mere mortals, we do not create, control, or own the artwork of God in another person's life—but we do get to enjoy it. Most of all, we can enjoy the traces of holiness left there by the divine Artist.

Among Jesus' last words on the cross were these: "It is finished."[4] He was referring, of course, to our salvation. It is accomplished, and we cannot add one single thing to the Lord's salvation in our own lives or in the lives of others. Imagine going to the Louvre and looking at one of the world's great masterpiece paintings. It would be absurd to say, "You know, that's pretty good, but I just need to add a little more red to it and it'll be perfect." You would ruin it. It's finished. And so is the art God has given you to behold in the lives of those around you. Just because you didn't contribute to the creativity doesn't mean that it isn't a masterpiece.

CRACKED CISTERNS

Most of the problems we create for ourselves in life, and virtually all of the problems we create in our relationships, are born out of anxiety. And the thing that usually gives us the most anxiety is the possibility that tomorrow will be worse than today. So we are constantly trying to "fix up" ourselves and our loved ones before anything gets worse. But the more desperately we try to make improvements, the more we tend to distort the creativity of God.

I'm not certain we are expected to ever find wholeness in this life, and I know we are not going to find it in another person. As the story of Adam and Eve reminds us, when humankind was created God placed the man and woman in a garden with something forbidden in the midst of it. Every day, when Adam and Eve walked by the tree of the knowledge of good and evil, they had to remember they were never created to have it all. There is always something missing in life. This is, in fact, the mark of a created being, for only God is whole and complete, lacking nothing. The missing part of our lives can either drive us crazy to the point where we lose paradise by reaching for more than we currently possess, or it can become the best altar for our prayers, where we remind ourselves of our dependence on God. When we understand how dependent we really are, we become free to enjoy the rest of the garden, as well as the people inside it, without trying to make them into our savior.

The life we have received has come to us only by the grace of God that flows down from heaven. This grace has brought us everything we really cherish in life. It's not very difficult to recognize this truth and to be grateful for it; the challenge is to believe that this sacred river will continue to flow tomorrow.

If we have faith in the faithfulness of the Supplier of the eternal river, we can enjoy life as an unfolding drama of grace. If we don't, we will waste our days trying to collect living water, just in case the river dries up. We will try to hoard all the love, money, power, and security we can find. As the prophet Jeremiah once observed, nothing could make God angrier. Why? Because we have reached the point where our little stash has become our god—a god that leaks:

> Be appalled, O heavens, at this,
>> be shocked, be utterly desolate,
>>> says the LORD,
> for my people have committed two evils:
>> they have forsaken me,
> the fountain of living water,
>> and dug out cisterns for themselves,
> cracked cisterns
>> that can hold no water.[5]

When we turn away from the fountain of living water and begin to build cisterns, as if we could save the water and ensure tomorrow, we find that we have lost everything we were once trying to save. Love certainly doesn't store up very well. If you save it, you lose it; if you give it away, you get it back. The same is true for money, power, and mission, whether or not we admit it. None of these things has a shelf life. So we must spend it all today, every ounce of love and energy, believing that there will be more tomorrow when we need it. Even our money must be given back to God as a daily discipline of asking him to use it as he sees fit. The day we start to hoard it is the day we begin investing in leaky cisterns.

The point of living water isn't to save it, but to enjoy it.

I once invited a wealthy elderly man with no heirs to start giving away some of his money before he died. By doing so he could reap the enjoyment of seeing the world of good it would do. However, in spite of having more money than several small nations, he was still worried about the volatility of his own life. At one point, he hesitated, "Well, you just never know." In that moment I knew the kingdom of God would never see a cent of his money. He was using it all to collect life in a cracked cistern that would let his health leak out day by day until it was finally gone.

He was right when he told me that we just never know about the future. Instead of being a cause for anxiety, however, this reality can be a source of adventure. We are always free to respond to the mystery of life by choosing to believe that God will take care of us tomorrow—and that he may bring something even better into our lives. Who knows? That's the adventure of planting our lives next to the flowing rivers of living water.

The river, remember, is the Holy Spirit, who proceeds from the Father and Son into our parched souls. When we show up thirsty tomorrow at the well, the Spirit will still be there to satisfy our longing and to bring us home again to the Father's house, where resides all the security and love any mortal could ever dare hope for. The Spirit's ministry is always to adopt us into the Son's relationship with the Father, so that we are always beloved sons and daughters in this house. Jesus prepared a place for us there, and the Spirit gives it to us. We will still get to have it tomorrow—and even for an eternity of tomorrows.

When we rest in this discovery, which is what faith permits, we are set free from futilely clinging to relationships and other things and expecting them to take care of us tomorrow. Better yet, we are set free to spend our days pointing the thirsty souls around us to the sacred river.

Each day, as we renew our adopted identity in the midst of the triune fellowship of Father, Son, and Spirit, we remember that our purpose in life is to glorify this God and to enjoy him forever. We glorify him not by developing our own reservoir of security, but by becoming a tributary of his love to the world around us. We enjoy him in exactly the same way. In other words, our passions become an expression of the passion of Christ, who gave everything so that others might know the joy he knew—the joy of being "the beloved."

SURPRISING GOD

As we come to accept our total dependence on God, ironically we discover that we subsequently receive our freedom. Not only are we free from our fear of not having enough, free to behold beauty, and free from manipulating others into meeting our needs, we are also free from our familiar mission of trying to climb our way back into heaven by means of a carefully lived life.

The holy river of living water only flows from heaven down to earth. It does not matter how frantically we paddle our way upstream, we will never evade and overcome the torrents of grace that insist on flowing toward the earth. All we can do is gratefully receive the refreshment to our souls as it comes.

Actually, there is one other thing we can do: We can play a bit in the waters of life. The Teacher of the book of Ecclesiastes instructs us, "Go, eat your bread with enjoyment, and drink your wine with a merry heart; for God has long ago approved what you do."[6] This wonderful, but typically overlooked, verse ought to be remembered when we are begging God for direction but hearing nary a word from him. Maybe he has already approved our choices.

When people talk to me about some momentous choice they are facing, they generally make it clear that they are seeking God's will. So we talk about the options, search Scripture for clues, and pray for direction. Should she take the job or not? Should he marry her or wait a little longer? Should they have children or not? "Please tell us, Lord." After we finish praying, there is usually still no burning bush or burning conviction. As these folks leave my office, I often wonder if perhaps God hasn't put his hands in his pockets, shrugged his shoulders, and said, "It doesn't really matter either way, because I love you."

If God wants us to get to a certain place in life or have a certain companion along the way, we won't be able to miss it. Remember, though, God is a lot more concerned about *who* we are than *where* we get to, or even who our companions are along the way. His invitation to us is to spend a lot more time praying to know his heart than his will. Of course, as we draw closer to his passionate love for us, we are changed—which is, after all, always his will. Everything else is a free expression of gratitude.

When my daughter was a little girl, I took special delight in the presents she would give me. It didn't matter that she bought the gift with my money or used my wrapping paper to wrap it or rode to the store in my car to get it. I was still filled with joy to open the present and receive a symbol of her love for me. But the best part, every time, was looking into her eyes as she saw my delight. I delighted in her delight! So, too, it doesn't matter where we work, or with whom we establish a relationship, or how we try to package our lives—it all belongs to the Father anyway. It still gives him enormous joy when we eat our food with joy and drink our wine with a merry heart, simply because he delights in our delight.

In the novel *Mariette in Ecstasy*, Ron Hansen introduces us to a young woman as she is applying to a convent to become a nun.

Entering this convent has been the goal of Mariette's life from the time she was a young girl. She wants so much to do the right thing with her life, and she is convinced that "the right thing" means settling into the devout, regimented life of the convent. But after her arrival, she falls too deeply in love with Jesus Christ. She finds joy in what should be hardship. She also prays differently from the other nuns, focusing not on her prayers but on the One to whom she is praying. Her relationship with God becomes too powerful to be contained by the careful routines of monastic life.

Eventually she even bears the wounds (the stigmata) of the crucified Christ on her body, which is just too much for the other nuns to take. So she is kicked out of the convent because of her excesses in piety. The expulsion is devastating to her. She feels disgraced, exiled into the parched wilderness.

Thirty years later, she writes a letter to the convent, describing what she has learned about a world so full of God's mystery. In the closing lines of the letter she observes:

> We try to be formed and held and kept by him, but instead
> he offers us freedom. And now when I try to know his will,
> his kindness floods me, his great love overwhelms me, and
> I hear him whisper, "Surprise me."[7]

When we have become convinced that we are the beloved of the Father, the whole world opens up to us as an opportunity to express our gratitude. Our many choices about jobs, relationships, and ministries are never more than ways of selecting wrapping paper for the life we present as a surprising gift to God. It just doesn't matter much how we choose to make the gift. What matters is the identity of the person who is making the gift.

Have you embraced your identity as the beloved—the Father's gift to you? That's what matters. That's the "will of God." And it is the only thing that will satisfy your thirst.

UNFINISHED ENDING

Do you ever wonder what happened when Jesus left the Samaritan town of Sychar, where he had met the woman at the well? Did the woman marry the man she had been living with? After Jesus' conversation with the woman, he spent two days with the people of Sychar; they then came to believe in him as "the Savior of the world." But does this mean that the people in the city reconciled with the woman and began to treat her more graciously? Did she now have friends to go with her to the well? We don't know.

Like many of the stories in the Gospels, this one seems unfinished. Maybe that's the point. After the people of Sychar saw Jesus with them, anything was possible in that town. Now it is up to those who have seen the Savior to finish the story.

You are the beloved. Anything is possible.

NOTES

Chapter One: Our Parched Souls

1. See Psalm 42:1
2. See 2 Kings 17:24–41
3. The Samaritans actually had a long-standing feud with respect to the temple. When Zerubbabel, Jeshua, and the people sought to rebuild the temple after the two southern tribes of Judah had returned from captivity in Babylon (see Ezra 3:8–9), the Samaritans offered to help but were rejected (see Ezra 4:1–5). So they began to actively work against the temple and later became the enemies of Nehemiah. By the time Jesus was born, the animosity between the Jews and Samaritans was deeply rooted.
4. See John 4:1–42
5. Cited in Russell Shorto, "Belief by the Numbers," *New York Times Magazine* (7 December 1997), 60–61.
6. Ruth Shalit, "Quality Wings," *The New Republic* (20 July 1998), 24–31.
7. M. Craig Barnes, *When God Interrupts: Finding New Life Through Unwanted Change* (Downers Grove, Ill.: InterVarsity Press, 1996).
8. Richard Ford, *The Sportswriter* (New York: Vintage Books, 1986), 83.
9. See Philippians 1:6
10. John 4:13–14
11. Cited in *Religion Today*, www.ReligionToday.com, September 30, 1999.

Chapter Two: Right Answers Aren't Enough

1. 1 Corinthians 11:29–30 KJV
2. See Matthew 28:20
3. John 4:27
4. The story is found in Acts 10:1–48.
5. Conversation paraphrased from Acts 10:13–15
6. Acts 10:2
7. See Acts 15:7–11
8. Abraham Lincoln, "Second Inaugural Address," quoted in Sidney E. Ahlstrom, *A Religious History of the American People* (New Haven, Conn.: Yale University Press, 1972), 687.

9. Psalm 27:4

Chapter Three: A Stranger in Community

1. See Luke 15:17
2. John 6:66
3. John 6:68
4. Simone Weil, *Waiting for God* (New York: Putnam's, 1951), 69.
5. Ursula Hegi, *Stones from the River* (New York: Simon & Schuster, 1997), 336.
6. Matthew 22:10

Chapter Four: When Prayer Dries Up

1. Anne Lamott, *Traveling Mercies: Some Thoughts on Faith* (New York: Random House, 1999), 82.
2. James 5:16 KJV
3. Matthew 27:46
4. Joan Chittister, OSB, *Wisdom Distilled from the Daily: Living the Rule of St. Benedict Today* (San Francisco: HarperSanFrancisco, 1991), 37.
5. See Acts 12:1–5, 12–17
6. John Claypool, *Tracks of a Fellow Struggler* (Waco, Tex.: Word, 1974), 76–77.
7. Mark 14:33–34
8. Mark 14:36
9. Luke 5:16, emphasis added
10. 2 Corinthians 2:17

Chapter Five: Compassion Fatigue

1. John 1:3
2. Colossians 1:16–17
3. Philippians 1:6
4. See Mark 9:14–29
5. See Mark 3:15; 6:7
6. Mark 9:18
7. William J. Bennett, *The Index of Leading Cultural Indicators: Facts and Figures on the State of American Society* (New York: Simon & Schuster, 1994), 72, 78–79.
8. Mark 9:24
9. See Acts 1:8
10. Mark 9:29
11. See Karl Barth, *The Christian Life* (Grand Rapids: Eerdmans, 1981), 171–73.
12. John 6:5
13. John 6:9
14. John 6:11 NIV

Chapter Six: It's Not About You

1. John 4:19 RSV
2. Ephesians 1:3
3. See Ephesians 1:13
4. Romans 8:15–17
5. James Torrance, *Worship, Community, and the Triune God of Grace* (Downers Grove, Ill.: InterVarsity Press, 1996), 30.
6. See John Calvin, *Institutes of the Christian Religion*, vol. 1, bk. II, ch. xvii, ed. John T. McNeill (Philadelphia: Westminster, 1960), 528–34.
7. Romans 12:2

Chapter Seven: The Searching God

1. See Henri, Nouwen, *Making All Things New* (San Francisco: Harper & Row, 1981), especially 65–80.
2. See John 6:35; 7:37–38; 8:12
3. John 8:25
4. John 8:29
5. Mark 1:35; 6:31
6. Psalm 56:8
7. See Exodus 33:12–23
8. Isaiah 6:5
9. Luke 1:12
10. Luke 1:29–30
11. See Luke 1:63
12. See Luke 2:18
13. See Luke 2:33
14. Luke 1:18
15. Matthew 3:15
16. Matthew 3:17
17. 1 Peter 1:16; see also Leviticus 11:45
18. Exodus 26:34; see also Hebrews 9:3
19. See John 2:19; see also Matthew 26:59–61
20. See Romans 14:5–6, 20; Galatians 4:10–11; 1 Timothy 4:4–5; Colossians 1:15–20
21. See 1 Peter 2:5, 9
22. For a fuller treatment of the presence of Gnosticism in some forms of evangelical Christianity, see Michael Horton, *In the Face of God* (Dallas: Word, 1996).
23. Isaiah 6:3
24. Luke 19:38
25. Luke 19:39
26. Luke 19:40
27. Luke 19:44

Chapter Eight: Communing with God

1. See Acts 1:9–12
2. Acts 1:6
3. Luke 24:49
4. Acts 2:4
5. Philippians 1:21
6. See Genesis 2:10
7. Psalm 1:3
8. Isaiah 35:6
9. See Revelation 22:1–6
10. John 7:37–39
11. Psalm 34:8
12. Acts 1:5
13. See Acts 1:13–14
14. Matthew 6:6
15. See Acts 1:18–19
16. See John 13:30
17. See Acts 1:21–26
18. Luke 24:38
19. 1 John 4:18
20. Galatians 2:20
21. Romans 8:14, 17

Chapter Nine: The Longing to Confess

1. See Acts 4:34–37
2. See Acts 5:1–11
3. Dennis Prager, "The Sin of Forgiveness," *The Wall Street Journal* (15 December 1997).
4. See Matthew 3:5
5. Luke 3:9, 18
6. Luke 3:7
7. Luke 3:10
8. Romans 7:15, 25
9. See Romans 7:21
10. See 1 Peter 5:8
11. Romans 7:24–25
12. See the story in John 11
13. James 3:6
14. John 11:43
15. John 4:20. The Greek word for *you* here is plural.
16. John 4:23–24
17. See, for example, John 1:14; 14:6
18. See the story of David and Bathsheba in 2 Samuel 11

Chapter Ten: The Courage to Believe

1. See Matthew 5:43–48
2. See Matthew 10:39; Luke 9:24–25; 17:33
3. See Luke 5:1–11
4. Luke 5:6–7
5. Luke 5:8
6. Luke 5:10
7. Augustine, *The Confessions of Saint Augustine*, trans. R. S. Pine-Coffin (Middlesex, England: Penguin Books, 1961), 164.
8. Augustine, *Confessions*, 169.
9. John 14:6
10. Augustine, *Confessions*, 176.
11. See John 20:3–23
12. See John 20:25
13. See John 11:16; 20:24
14. John 20:27–29
15. See Psalm 1:3
16. Fred Craddock, "Faith 'Because of' and 'In Spite of'," *The Living Pulpit* 1, no. 2 (April–June 1992), 19.

Chapter Eleven: Finding a Holy People

1. Charles Krauthammer, "Beware the Study of Turtles," *Time* (28 June 1993), 76.
2. Caligula was a notoriously licentious emperor of Rome from A.D. 37–41.
3. See John 4:28–29
4. See Deuteronomy 5:9–10
5. For an extended study of the differences between ancient and modern families, see Rodney Clapp, *Families at the Crossroads: Beyond Traditional and Modern Options* (Downers Grove, Ill.: InterVarsity Press, 1993).
6. Matthew 12:50
7. See Romans 8:12–17; Galatians 3:26–4:7
8. Summarized from Dietrich Bonhoeffer, *Life Together*, trans. John Doberstein (New York: Harper & Row, 1954), 26–27.
9. See Romans 8:17
10. 1 Corinthians 9:24
11. Numbers 11:4; Ezekiel 23:42
12. See Luke 10:25–37
13. Luke 19:10

Chapter Twelve: Finding a Holy Place

1. John 1:36
2. See John 1:38
3. John 1:39

4. See Luke 13:24
5. Luke 18:25
6. See 1 Corinthians 1:27; see also 1 Corinthians 4:10
7. 1 Peter 1:1
8. Psalm 137:1–4
9. Psalm 119:64
10. See Mark 9:2–13; Matthew 4:1–11; John 2:13–22
11. 1 Corinthians 3:17
12. 1 Peter 2:5
13. Jeremiah 29:11
14. Jeremiah 29:5–7
15. Luke 9:51, 57
16. See Acts 9:1–9; Matthew 4:21–22; John 4:7
17. Luke 9:57
18. See Revelation 21:2, 4
19. See Luke 9:60, 62

Chapter Thirteen: Finding a Holy Purpose

1. John 4:38
2. Luke 4:18–19
3. See Genesis 12:2–3
4. See Luke 4:30
5. See 1 Samuel 2:12–25; 3:11–14
6. 1 Samuel 3:1
7. Amos 5:21, 23–24
8. John 19:19
9. See Ephesians 5:8–16
10. See Augustine, *City of God* (New York: Modern Library, 2000).
11. See Luke 10:18–19; John 8:42–47
12. Matthew 10:34
13. Exodus 2:14
14. See Acts 9:19–25
15. Ephesians 6:12 KJV
16. See, for example, Matthew 7:28–29; see also Luke 4:32

Chapter Fourteen: Finding a Holy Joy

1. John 4:29
2. Psalm 31:7
3. Zephaniah 3:14–15, 17
4. See Frederick Buechner, *The Magnificent Defeat* (San Francisco: HarperSanFrancisco, 1985), 90.
5. See Matthew 10:29; 19:13–15; Mark 5:24–34
6. See John 2:1–11; 11:33–35
7. Zephaniah 1:12
8. Revelation 3:15–16

9. Revelation 3:17
10. Haggai 1:6
11. See Matthew 13:45–46
12. See Matthew 25:14–30
13. Revelation 1:8
14. See Genesis 12:1–5
15. See Genesis 16:1–4
16. Genesis 17:5
17. Genesis 17:15–17
18. Genesis 18:13–14
19. See Genesis 17:19
20. See Genesis 17:20

Chapter Fifteen: Finding a Holy Self

1. Psalm 25:14
2. John 15:15
3. See John 7:38–39
4. John 19:30
5. Jeremiah 2:12–13
6. Ecclesiastes 9:7
7. Ron Hansen, *Mariette in Ecstasy* (New York: HarperCollins, 1991), 179.